CW01509211

TO DEAR

MARIAN

LOVE

DANNY

A Nazzy
House Boy

Danny Warren

Copyright © 2022 by Danny Warren.

All rights reserved. No part of this publication may be reproduced, distributed, or transmitted in any form or by any means, including photocopying, recording, or other electronic or mechanical methods, without the prior written permission of the author, except in the case of brief quotations embodied in critical reviews and certain other noncommercial uses permitted by copyright law.

Printed in the United States of America.

Library of Congress Control Number: 2022950730

ISBN	Paperback	979-8-88887-009-9
	Hardback	979-8-88887-010-5
	eBook	979-8-88887-011-2

Westwood Books Publishing LLC
Atlanta Financial Center
3343 Peachtree Rd NE Ste 145-725
Atlanta, GA 30326

www.westwoodbookspublishing.com

CONTENTS

Introduction

Misery and loss will always remain as unwelcome bedfellows in this most dreadful of lifetime scenarios. World war has finally come to its close in Europe and the year is 1945: The only abiding legacy from all of this horror is the emotional one that meant that millions of disrupted family lives would be savaged as a result, many of them due to unfortunate histories that have taken longer than time itself, to heal.

Picture, if you will the circumstances that involved one young mother placing her two-week old child into the care of anonymous authority figures for the purpose of his future well-being, knowing in that one dreadful moment, that she is giving her child away; a little child that grew and nourished within her own body; one that she grew to both treasure and love; an integral part of her own exclusive self and a part of her own individual consciousness.

It is hard to imagine those conditions that existed in the year of 1945: The world had been at war for much too long and it was finally attempting to readjust itself, with all of the emotional and financial consequences that that was likely to involve, conspiring for all of that time, to engender a multitude of increasingly difficult survival decisions for most people, and to impose those same nefarious implications on all of the various aspects of life that would have negatively stimulated normal home life, but most importantly, would have had an unexpected and adverse effect on the particular life of one young pregnant woman in particular.

In this narrative the writer will attempt to describe, in his own words, the story of his own experiences in growing up as an infant child, impressed through no fault of his own into a system of care that he had never had any choice about: He will attempt to explain what the implications of those experiences meant to him during the perpetuation of his young life. He will attempt, finally, to relate the influences of that life into his own personal development: He will also attempt to explain the impact that this whole situation has had on the rest of his young life: He was placed, for his pain into a regime that was maintained with the implementation of an enforced culture system; one that ended up failing him totally, on a personal level, while at the same time catering to his more essential and personal needs, with an essentially carefree indifference.

This is a story about a child who was placed, not from choice, into a strange home, but it will remain, of necessity, an anecdotal tale rather than one of mere fiction, or indeed any other kind of literary relevance whatsoever.

Memories are such liars when they feed on the distractions of fragile and promising imaginations: We have always to be aware of the dangers that exist when we start to believe that false memories might actually have been a kind of reality all of the time: I have therefore taken the greatest of care to ensure that the facts that I have presented in this narrative are as true, accurate and unembellished as they possibly can be, to the best of my memory, knowledge and belief and where there may perhaps be embellishments that have been included in this account, that might lead me to suppose that certain details may not have been truly representative, or otherwise unfairly coloured, those details will as a matter of course, be removed from the final text.

This tale might chafe with many readers, at the telling, but it is not intended in any way to anneal the harrowing exposes of lifetime experience that readers might have imagined them to be or even perhaps what it was that they had hoped that they might have been, in the first place, during the time that I was placed into the care of the nuns at

Nazareth house: Rather it aims to be as truthful as it can be, with all of the recollections that follow, as I am able to make them, without any inclusions of adjectival colouration, or just any plain exaggerations that might ultimately affect the accuracy of the text in one form or another: So please, dear reader, if you do find this narrative distressing, do please keep it in mind that these were events that all happened a long time ago and many of the stories that I am recounting here won't be that different from many other events that may have been encountered by many other different people, in many other different homes, from those that I am relating to, here today.

This writer has attempted, with the best of his memory and ability to recount the experiences during the time that he lived at Nazareth house, up to the age of fifteen years when he was finally discharged from the care of the nuns, but also to transcribe as well as he is able to, the story of those events as he remembers them, during that time, on to paper: Related anecdotes may have been added, simply to add some imagery to the scene, but where this is the case, they will have been included only so that the reader might divine some differences of colour and impact in the story that might otherwise have affected the perception of the content of this tale, as a whole: It is important after all, that sympathetic readers who might have had similar experiences to the ones that are recounted on these pages, in their own lives, might yet find within themselves an affinity with memories of their own, that they might then be able to relate to, in their own lives; then perhaps they might gain some solace from reading these stories as well: They might even come to realise that their own message is being heard in the same breath, and to a similar degree, as the one that has been presented on these pages: These events have had considerable relevance on many aspects of my life, that have progressed beyond the experiences while I lived at Nazareth house and they have all left lasting implications for me in the learning process that involved coping with all of my own recurring complications, as well as in all of the future attempts at coexistence with my fellow man, that followed them.

A closing comment that is worthy of mention concerns the ongoing season that is consequences: I often wonder whether, with the very best of her convictions and dispositions, my mother would have nursed some doubts about the validity of her decision of placing me in the care of the nuns. If institutions had not been the places that depended on the enforcement of control as their tool of regulation, there might at least have been concerns in some places, that maybe the strictures and regulations that enforced that authority culture might not, at the end of the day, have been the kindest and most positive outcome for any child, and possibly not the best preparation for him either, when he was finally released into the coarser reality that became his life beyond those walls.

CHAPTER 1

Arrival

I was placed into the care of the organisation of nuns called THE POOR SISTERS OF NAZARETH at the age of two weeks: There is little that I can ably record of the personal history of that time that I can reliably relate to, concerning this particular period of my life. The purpose of any questions or functions that might have been part of any decision made at that time in my name, will probably serve little of meaningful purpose either. Conjecture about the why's and the wherefores of events that led to the evolution of any of the decisions at this time in my life, will still be as pointless, at the end of the day, as the distribution of any kind of blame for the consequences of any of those decisions, in any of the subsequent years.

The first Nazareth house home in which I stayed was in a place called Criccieth, in Wales, and the year was 1946: All of these convent homes are named as NAZARETH HOUSE'S and they all belong to the same order of nuns: The homes all carry identical names, all called 'Nazareth house': I obviously did not realise it at the time but I was destined to spend the bulk of my formative years living among these people until I was 15 years old: There were many other homes like this one, run by that same order of nuns, placed all over the world, all of them operated by the same religious order and all existing for the sole purpose of providing care to disadvantaged people, of whatever age and of whatever persuasion, religious or racial, that had been deprived of a fair opportunity in their own lives, so that they were required instead to endure subsequent indignities, whoever and whatever that might have involved: As an infant child, I have little enough to add regarding this period of my life since any recollection of events at that time would obviously have been flushed away by the occasional flattery of unengaged memory: Clearly, I would not have had any way of knowing, at such an infant age, that I would be placed into an environment bound by a strict culture of regulation and an inordinately strict control criteria, without ever having a single idea about what it was that that future was actually likely to involve, that I might have been confronted with, in my new and rarefied future: Due to my young age and my limited life experience, it would hardly have seemed to me to be that different a place from any of the environments that I might well have known of hitherto. (One might reasonably suppose that recollections of previous pasts, albeit parental ones, might even have related them to earlier fabric moments that I might have been able to enjoy with my mother.) so that even at this very young age, the anticipation and adventure that these changes might have represented for me, suggested elements of anticipation to me, when I eventually arrived for the first time at my new address. In the rarefied culture into which I was to be so rigorously impressed, any pain of speculation promised only hesitancy within this early life imposition, embedding it with a latent anticipation that at the end of the day, all might finally be well: At the very least I was perhaps guilty of childishly optimistic speculation: That any child, at such a young age, might have been expected to be aware of a situation that was not fully of his own natural expectations or even of his own personal needs, particularly regarding any confusions that might still have persisted regarding parenthood and all of the trappings that constituted reality, up to that moment, would be as fanciful as supposing that any adaptation to new life conditions could be taken to as readily as a duck takes to its water.

At the age of five years, I was transferred to another different convent; one that was located in Southend, also run and operated by the same order of nuns. I am 5 years older now and the year is 1951: It was at my new home in Southend that I spent the remainder of these formative years. It constituted the genesis of an existence that in no way prepared me for the life into which I was to be so unceremoniously impressed, for the remainder of the time that I would be required to spend in the care of these people.

Unsurprisingly, I have scant recollections of those early years so that I am not able to dwell on any of the specifics of my early life in that new place: All I can do is to propose, based purely on the ease with which I was able to adapt to this new world anyway, that it was certainly due as much as anything to my young age: In purely practical terms I had been enabled to adjust to the new life in Southend, and it probably extenuated the personal and emotional adjustment that must have begun for me while I was living in Criccieth. Any harsh assessment would suggest that adaptions to any life away from parents cannot have been the easiest one for me to deal with and the intrinsic complexities of any separation must have been, in actuality, the most gut wrenching and soul destroying of experiences ever to have been inflicted on what would have been, at the time, as an emotionally conflicted child.

The Nazareth house that I moved to from Wales was located on the London road in Southend, Essex: It was a large, red and imposing (or so it seemed to me) structure and I recall being impressed by its size at the time, the moment that I passed through the large green gates that also served as the main entrance to the driveway and the house. Included in its population were infants who all lived in a separate section of the house and that was presumably also the place where I would begin living my life here: About sixty older children also occupied the main part of the building and a number of other people of more advanced years ('old' people) also kept to their own living area, separated from everybody else: The grounds were thankfully large and there was no shortage of space within the perimeter for children to play in and recreate.

In the course of this story I will attempt to explore the circumstances that led to the disposal of this child into the ministrations of a group of people endowed with all of the well-meaning sensitivity of inadequately uneducated disciplinarians, whose only function in life seemed to revolve around the control of people who had wanted nothing more from life than a freedom to attain normal life function and positive purpose: With the added benefit of kindness and sincere intention, blessed with a more positive determination than 'normal', children might well have achieved a level of purpose that would have been altogether more appropriate to their state of general well-being: To appreciate the validity of that statement, we need to be able to see for ourselves the desperation and the hunger of children who will seize at any avenue of unrequited affection, from whatever source it can be found, with an unrelenting sincerity: Sadly, however it remained simply as a medium of control that remained the normal pattern of emotional stipulation, throughout the extension of these young lives; A fact that remained particularly true when applied to children that lived at Nazareth house: The primary function of the nuns, as far as I was able to perceive it to be, was to ensure that the path along which the children would be guided would be the one that was most appropriate to the general requirement of the nuns themselves and they would always be directed by the doctrine's and creeds of their religious order: I cannot begin to imagine the pain and the anguish that was felt by parents who had had to hand over a child that they had carried within their own bodies for fully nine months: To have to live with the knowledge that they might never see that child, ever again, but also perhaps to suspect as well, that they were condemning that child to a life as different and unexpected as the one that they might well have, in a different time and in different circumstances, been fortunate enough to have been able to bring them up themselves, in any case.

The popularly employed use of language such as words like 'orphan' (which was the context in which I always felt that it always applied to the children at Nazareth house) always seemed to me to be something of a discredited misnomer, in most cases: It seemed as if it was employed normally, as a comfortably generalised description for any child who has, apparently never had a parent of his own, whether due to personal tragedy, or because of some other misfortune, and who would therefore have been found to be in need of support as a result: I always believed that all orphans were children who had actually lost parents, due to some unfortunate demise in their lives, in which case a reunion would have been out of the question in any case: As it was, many of the children that lived at Nazareth house actually did have parents that were still alive and it came as a surprise to me as well that a good number of those parents actually returned, in the fullness of time, to reclaim their children once again, after the children had grown that bit older: It did however indicate to me that the all prevailing purpose of the nuns was never to turn a child away, whatever their circumstances, if they were ever in need of care and protection: I could never have accused them of being judgemental about agreeing to take anybody in, that was ever considered to be in need of care.

Later in life, I learned that my Mother had always insisted that I be given a name that had always been her own personal favourite and also that both of my parent's names should be placed on my birth certificate: While it is a fact that I have little knowledge of any of the consequences regarding details relating to my parents lives, it is comforting to me to know that they did attach some significance to the importance of assuring that the details provided on my birth certificate were complete and accurate: Of this much information, I am happy to depend: I spent a great deal of time wondering, not unreasonably, about information that might have been related to my mother, but whenever I tried to discover anything of that nature, it is always on the principle that I still remained detached about the whole 'parent' thing: I had after all, been placed into a time frame that had excluded any recollections concerning my mother as a living person, or indeed, even excluding any possibility of a future that I might ever have been likely to spend with her, now or at a later time: I do not own any personal items that might have enabled me to know what she had actually looked like, in my past: Blasé acceptances of any familiarity conditions suggest that I was required to adapt to this situation accordingly, and to these prevailing circumstances, so that a need for questions of any kind became increasingly less relevant with the insistent passage of time: Intrinsic acceptances of all of the unrequited variables concerning my family actually gave me little of comfort, and the ravages of this unnecessarily cruel singularity might hopefully have been alleviated somewhat with the enduring passage of septic time: I would adapt, eventually, of course, to this new life at Nazareth house, even with the added vagary of qualified memory impositions, labouring always to make those real voices heard, yet receiving little of meaningful comfort or restitution that might alleviate any misgivings, in the long term. Small comfort is the need to understand the forces that have always been in play, cultivating these sorry processes and gaining immediate prominence within these oh so unusual circumstances: Inherent insecurity, that was always of its time, and the rigours of harsher economic realities, did not bode well however, for the future well-being of one of this nation's erstwhile war babies!

There were a large number of Nazareth house institutions dotted across the world at this time and it is not difficult to imagine that if these homes each housed some fifty to sixty children, that must have meant that there were many more dispossessed children passing into similar limbos of uncertainty, much like my own: One is inclined to suppose that there must have been opportunities for many kinds of abuse, as well, in varying degrees, to many of those unfortunate inmates, in many of those homes: Sadly, no recourse to outside help or protection was ever been made available to any of them, since the culture of protection for children did not even exist at that time, that might actually have provided for some semblance of safer and more secure environment conditions: The abiding care structure that was supposed to be the purpose of overseeing communities, might have enabled those inequalities to be rectified in a relatively short order: Perhaps, with a little more imagination, it should not be too difficult either, to suppose that the situation in some of those institutions would not have been that different in those times, all those years ago: We can only hope that the histories of those places remain as the redundant scars of an unacceptable past, and that those same memories can be comfortably erased, without too much damage being inflicted, at the end of the day.

This is not a tale that attempts to engender anger or recrimination, though heaven knows why that should not be the case when considering the lot of so many of the children that were actually delivered into these homes; unworthy substitutes for the stories of their own broken lives: But as I stated earlier, if anger and adjectives had been incorporated into this tale, they would only generate negative emotional reactions in this sadly monochrome dissertation and that will not serve the greater need of providing enquiring minds with a truer understanding of the activities that usually passed for stability in these places: Institutions by their very nature are common feeding grounds for many different kinds of abuse and are heaven sent havens for those who are the practitioners of them: They are encouraged to exist within these zones of indifference and insecurity because of the ready availability of endlessly hopeless and helpless human fodder: I cannot pretend that that was not a situation that is recalled in any extreme, by this writer: Undoubtedly excesses were perpetrated with unbecoming regularity as a matter of course, on all of the inmates in their more private moments, but apart from the stock-in trade preference for unreasonable behaviour that has always been prevalent when people are enabled to live together in a close proximity, it does becomes a more normal circumstance in the lonely stricture that is real life: I am unable to recall a moment however, when it approached the more dangerous levels that are popularly considered as being extreme or excessive, but that is not to say that such circumstances have never existed for me.

At the risk of repetition this writer emphasises that this story is not intended to disparage in any way, the work of the 'poor sisters' but only to outline the complications that are unavoidably inherent in any system that involves this form of regulation, utilised mainly as a means of control, particularly one as conformal as this one regrettably was. It is unavoidable that these institutions, by their very nature are always likely to succumb to the many forms of rigour, imposed, that by so doing, they might ably function more efficiently as a result: Unfortunately, with efficiency comes a level of control that will always feed on itself, with the abiding endorsement of those same rules, and as with all kinds of regulation, when that kind of stipulation is allowed to occur, a singular abuse is never very far behind.

Sadly, the residue that was the final outcome of many of these wasted lives involved abuse in various forms, both violent and sexual, when they were operated within the confines of an institutional regime: A terrible stain that has been inflicted on those children, that will continue to plague them all with scores that will become, eventually their new necessity, when they do finally leave these homes for the last time.

CHAPTER 2

'Nazareth house' Criccieth was the home where everything of significance in my future really began to evolve for me; that whole caring thing! Memories are necessarily vague, regarding this period of my life: I was obviously much too small at that time, to realise that different options in my life might have offered me new alternatives that might have been more amenable to me; but then I imagine, I was just a happy-go lucky child without a care in the world, rather like any other youngster would have been, presented with what I could only assume was a new and exciting world of opportunity, laid out before me: I was probably comfortably receptive, in a childish sort of way, to what I would have seen as being a new reality existence: Vague memory cast-offs there must have been, to be sure, but how to deal with all of them must have depended, to a great extent, on what were the speculations that probably continued to plague me, even at that early age: I can only assume that those times must have been difficult for me during this period of transition, because of the emotional impact of events that had included an initial separation and any associated traumas that would have been involved, even then. It was perhaps easier for me to deal with the pain that I was having to engage with, if only at a subliminal level, by actually learning to cope with the whole thing in one way or another. Bland assertions among my 'betters' might have insisted that pain only be allowed to persist if it was able to serve a better purpose of maintaining the contention that stray thoughts and longings were better off left to be discharged in the fullness that was palliative time, locked away for ever from a lifetime never to come, of singular un-awareness and singular non-fulfilment: Maybe it was not such a bad thing, at the end of the day, that I perhaps opted to ignore this whole shallow scenario, subconsciously, as much as I was able to do, in the memory-mix up that must have been continually infesting this young life: This, after all, was all that remained of a lingering song that might have been better off discharged than saved at the end of the day, left finally to feed on the travesty that was this barren desert of emotional emptiness: It was probably not too long aftter this, that I finally came to understand the truth, that these latent experiences would soon invest me with the practice of strictly regulated daily life: Sharp shocks of daily activity would from henceforth become the radically new emotional mantra of the day: It would be naïve of me to assume that there might not have been emotional repercussions due to the separation from my mother and if I am truly honest with myself I have to concede that there might actually have been harrowing experiences that I subconsciously opted to dispel from memory altogether, rather than store them away against other more significant memory moments that might yet be resurrected in my future: That is not to suggest however that memory injuries do not develop permanent mental scars, expressed, albeit subconsciously, in patterns of behaviour of which I was perhaps, unaware at the time.

The more astute of my readers might suppose that any suggestion about my claims, that recollections of earlier years had actually been valid, might be related to those same claims of mistreatment, and the detrimental effects of turbulence during this early period of my life: All I can offer in defence of this particular conjecture is that even to this day, throughout this long life and even into this failing old age, the curse of hand tremors continue to plague me throughout most aspects of my everyday life, and the contention for this condition is that there might have been residual damage effects, due to earlier but unspecified life experiences.

There have been happier memories that I still recall: I still see myself seated in a pram in a leafy glade, surrounded by various other children, also seated in prams, and the song, 'Danny boy' being sung to me by my carers: Establishment in this environment at this young age, probably meant that an inordinate sense of confusion and adaptation may have contributed substantially to the overall adjustment that I was required to make, to my new environment. Such were the happier memories, rare as well as vague, but recollections nevertheless, that still linger in my mind; the dregs of bygone memories: Still it remains, this fodder that lingers as the shadow of a delinquent past, continuing to provide elements of comfort in the subliminal perception that is bygone time: Dearly do I hold on to all of these memories, while I am still able to, treasuring those memory smiles so as to embellish my mind with their vagrant needs and desires, even to this day. There are few enough of them that feed this hunger; perhaps a simple song that a heart can still lean on to for comfort, or a single memory moment that gives delight, if only for one subconscious moment, even today: Simple pleasures perhaps, but songs that still remain embroiled within the continuing maelstrom that is earlier happier thoughts.

Nazareth house, Criccieth was a convent that was blessed with its own large lawn at the front of the house on which the children were able to play, that spread across the whole front of the house: The only other fact that remains as being of any real interest to me, that I can still remember, is of a large wooden drum that all of the children used to play on, rolling it around between themselves, on the front lawn: As I told you, memories of this place are necessarily vague: What fun we must have had with that simple toy, even if it was in the earliest of times. Even now, few seemingly insignificant memories offer little of real comfort in terms of early childhood memories that seem to have lost all their sense of cognizance and relativity during my time in Criccieth: It seems to me that it remains just one more uninspiring aspect of a story with a lifeline that is of limited comprehension and of mutually amicable relationships, actually beginning for me as a life that I am destined to spend with these nuns: Yet I still cannot recall any other salient facts of significance about the place: I do recall that a large canvas tube was extended from one of the upper windows all the way down to the ground: The children would then be passed out of the window, to slide down the tube to the people waiting below: Fire escape practice, I presume! Whee!!!

Any allusion to life within the confines of Nazareth house, Criccieth will appear to the reader to be at the very least circumspect in relation to what are perceived as memory events and the recollection of possible occurrences within the home: I was certainly of an age at that time that I was bound actually to confer actual clarity, insofar as remembering anything of substance about the place was concerned; but of one fact I can be certain, I did live during this time in a convent in Wales for some five years and I can only hope that the period of tenure, in that place was generally amenable to me in terms of my treatment and my care and also of my ultimate well-being as well.

It is hard to imagine how I could have felt about all of these changes, and of how they actually affected my life, but innocence is an ungracious liar, particularly when there is so little of real knowledge that I might gainfully feed off, from it. If it had been supposed at the time that I would have been offered into the arms of this travesty of religious and mental control, for the remainder of my young life, I might then have viewed the whole prospect of my future development with rather more trepidation than I was actually prepared to do, at the time.

A venerable clergy man with whom I was to have a long and enduring relationship throughout my childhood, for reasons that I will elaborate upon later, was actually the person that I regarded as a kind and close familiar. He it was who delivered me by steam train from 'Nazareth house', Criccieth to my new and final home in Southend. I was aged five years by then and the year was 1951. I suspect that by then the period of final adjustment to the true reality of convent life had probably already materialised for me. I arrived eventually, at the infant nursery in Southend. The children would often meet, on occasion with this particular priest, Canon Bishop at regular intervals, as he waited outside the church for the children to come out, at the end of the service: He always made it his business to be waiting, to meet and greet all of the children: We, for our part, thought the world of him and we surrounded him with our unbridled attention. Friendship and kindness will always serve us as our emotional palliatives: We always addressed him as 'Farver'; an endearment that was employed by all of the children; as much as he continually tried to correct this nondescript abuse of the language, we just continued to crowd around him and mob him enthusiastically; always when the church service was finally over: I don't doubt that he probably enjoyed this attention from the children as much as they themselves did, hungering for any positive responses and for attention that was normally reciprocated by him as well: I believe that he was probably instrumental in many of the changes that led to the adjustments to the social and living conditions that eventually came into effect at Nazareth house, in the later years. For all of us he remained an emotional sanctuary that we could lean on for our own greedy comfort; We engaged with him hungrily on an emotional level. God bless you 'Farver', wherever you are! I always thought of his name as being an appropriate one for a person that I always substantially admired, certainly with the rabid perception that was one highly susceptible and emotionally receptive child: His correct title was: 'Reverend Canon Bishop', a catholic priest who served the local Catholic diocese, also including Nazareth house.

My time with the infants was pleasant of course as far as I am able to recall it: For infant children how could it not have been otherwise? The rigorous social demands that involved the future of social survival, was not yet ready to rear its ugly head at this moment in time: Perhaps there was a lingering awareness of emotional anomaly that I was not yet fully aware of, regarding my particular situation and a commensurate need to understand the implications or otherwise of those issues, but I did understand, even at that early age, that the importance of obedience and subservience, were 'necessities' that would always be appreciated and commended, at the end of the day: Perhaps also being unsure of my needs, and my becoming resigned to events that were beyond my control, must have been sufficient for me at the time, or perhaps it was just that I was learning to deal with it as a matter of course, even at that early stage in my development.

I was treated with kindness, to the best of my knowledge while I was in the infant's section: 'Mother Superior' called on us occasionally, at mealtimes, to distribute ha'pennies to the children: (easy to remember them as I still recall the sailing ships that were stamped on them.) I remember that they would also be immediately gathered up to be 'disappeared', as soon as she had gone.

There were, in total, thirty to thirty-five 'nuns' and one Mother superior that were resident in the convent: They all performed their regular duties that remained exclusive to that nun alone: Those duties were never performed by any other nun, other than the one that normally performed that duty, all of the time. The children were cared for exclusively by the same nuns, all of the time so that we always regarded them as our own personal authority figures but we always understood that one sister was exactly the same as the other when it came to the question of their individual authority status: All of the nuns were required to be obeyed with the same level of stipulation. The organisational running of the convent by the nuns remained very much a hierarchal premise so that 'Mother superior' maintained ultimate control throughout the whole of the local organisation and all the secondary orders of nuns, served all of the functions in the convent in their most familiar and regular fashion. Consequently, we were never really involved with any of the other nuns, at any other time: The nuns that looked after the children remained the nuns that looked after the children and they were the same ones that would be with us, day in and day out: They were always the same ones, remaining in charge of the children, and included engaging in any of the disciplinary practices that were deemed to be necessary at the time.

It was not too difficult to imagine how control of the children might be established, from their earliest age until the day that they actually left the home: The nuns were clothed in identical black robes; 'habits', that covered the whole of their bodies, from their heads all of the way down to their feet: It was not difficult also, to visualise them all as familiarly dominating spectral beings: Their authority was never questioned and they maintained their presence with a commanding menace and a confident self-assurance, as much because of their personally visual impact as it was because of their imposing demeanour and their stern and carefully cultivated presence: The manner of their appearance was never in any way different, from one day to the next and they were always clothed in exactly the same manner of appearance throughout the day. We always regarded them totally, as authority figures and we always reacted to them all, accordingly, in a similar manner.

The nuns performed their duties diligently, each day: One nun in particular still comes to mind: A small and aging person, effete but always so silent: Her name was Sister Mary Evangelista: All the nuns bore the name of the Virgin Mary, included as their very own second name (the middle name always being 'Mary') since they had ultimately elected to devote the rest of their lives to the service of the mother of God. They then adopted the name of a favoured saint as their chosen last name and retained that name as their own, for the remainder of their lives.

Sister Evangelista's duties involved maintaining all aspects of the 'laundry room' and her duties included the cleaning and preparing of the clothes and the bedding, ensuring that all of the items in the house were allocated to their correct locations and that all items of clothing and bedding were cleaned and correctly distributed, also to their correct location as well: I have to admit that I had never appreciated, at the time, the degree of dedication that must have been involved in the application of her tasks but also to admit that I do not recall any difficulties ever arising therefrom, out of the laundry department: She always performed her duties with a dedication that I found on reflection to be extraordinary: She beavered away dutifully and tirelessly at her task, day after day, from dawn to dusk!

Occasionally, a new nun would appear at the home, appointed occasionally I presume to help out with the children. They usually turned out to be nicer than the 'normal' nuns that looked after us on a regular basis. The new nuns seemed more inclined to show more compassion than we were normally accustomed to and seemed actually to enjoy the time that they spent taking care of us. It was certainly a more pleasant time for the children as well, as the new nuns seemed happy to interact with the children, and the children, for their part seemed to involve themselves more positively with the new nun at the same time. Sadly, nuns like this remained the exception rather than the rule, usually insisting that distance and rigid personal isolation always be maintained: As a rule they endeared themselves comfortably to the children, for the short time that they were with us: As a group we used to gather around them in a way that children might cling to a mother, demanding of any kind of attention: Perhaps we were inclined to cling to them rather more than was reasonable but who could ever have blamed the children for that; demanding of that particular company: Sadly, nuns like these never stayed with the children for very long and were 'vanished'; usually as promptly as they had arrived, fading finally away from the care of the children: After this sort of thing had happened more than the once, I grew, to accept the reality of the whole situation; that this was always the way that things were going to be and I eventually had to come to terms with the inevitability of it all, as well.

CHAPTER 3

Religion

Ah! That religion thing! The driving force that governed every issue of purpose and realty within the confines that was Nazareth house: It was, for all time and for ever the overriding constant that regulated all function within these walls: The prevailing repetition that was prayer and religious observance and were the devices that were rigorously maintained on a daily basis, and were themselves governed by the punctuality that was always habitual routine and the perpetually repetitive discipline that was the 'angelus' bell.

The bell was suspended from a central point in the house: It was a fairly loud bell with a long rope that hung all the way to the ground and could be reached through a conveniently placed window, three floors below. The availability and convenience of this bell meant that it could be operated with relative ease by any nun that happened to be passing by, at that moment. It always sounded precisely at the same time every day; at six o-clock in the morning and again at six o-clock each evening: It also rang again at twelve noon, also on each day: I imagine that it probably served as a reliable audible indicator for any of the local residents, living in the immediate vicinity, and also living within a comfortable listening distance of the home: The sound of the bell was audible in every location in the house, remaining as a constant source of comfort and recognition in the otherwise humdrum day-to-day routine that dictated all of life

17

within the place: On every period at which the bell rang, it sounded twelve times, signalling to the sisters that it was the moment, once more, for them to engage in a silent prayer: They carried for this purpose, on their person, an outsize string of beads around their waist, akin to a large rosary, with a crucifix attached to its end, with which they might then count off the statutory number of 'Hail Marys' as they recited the prayers in the privacy of their own minds. They also carried on their person, at all times and for the same purpose, a small prayer book, commonly referred to as the 'Office' to which they constantly referred, in their continual pursuit of a spiritual sustenance: I did sometimes wonder, since this routine of prayer was maintained so rigidly on the basis of trust, how easily it might have been possible for them to skip the odd page or two as they walked along, reading those daily passages to themselves: Like so many of my stranger ideas, it will probably pass the test of time as just one more fleeting fantasy, to be consigned eventually to a bin of distant memory games; forever to be pasted in the mists of vacant memory songs; but then again, why should I not to be denied an occasional mental chuckle?

The black 'habits' that all of the 'sisters' wore, at all times during the day, were of an identical pattern and design and included, as I have already said, long black garments that covered their bodies completely, from their heads right down to their feet, much in the fashion of some people in eastern countries: The outfits also incorporated a white hood that surrounded the face, enclosing it completely, so that the face itself seemed to be like some implanted, framed perception, modelled entirely within the hood: Occasionally, young novices came by to visit at the convent: We often watched them, surreptitiously, at a distance, playing loudly among themselves rather as young girls are inclined to do: Interestingly, they all arrived dressed in similar white gowns, identical in every way to the ones worn by normal nuns, but of all white, clearly so that they might readily be identified as novitiates, not yet fully integrated into the normal function that would eventually involve normal convent life. I rather expected them to be as stern and humourless as normal nuns apparently were: Perhaps, with time, they might even end up being cut from the same cloth as the rest of the nuns, but I earnestly hoped against hope, that at the end of the day, they would not! The novices all arrived at the convent, in the white 'habits' that they wore for the duration of their stay: It did cross my mind to wonder, at the time, whether they might actually change back into 'civvies' at some point in the proceedings, so that we might be able to discover what they did actually look like as normal people. The novices wore their habits presumably to declare to the world, their commitment to a lifetime of chastity and their dedication to the service of the Virgin Mary, for the rest of their lives. The power that the nuns were able to impose over the minds of them all, was both imperious and insidious and they all came to accept the essence of that authority and all of its religious connotations, without further question.

I must comment at this stage, while I am able to recall the times, on the levels of discipline that were sometimes exercised by some of the nuns on various occasions, but by one nun in particular, who remained in charge of the children for most of the time that I lived in the home: I have since discovered that she has been elevated to the position of Mother Superior, involving her in the supervision and overall operation of a convent in some other place: There was however one activity that she, in particular, took particular delight in inflicting on the boys: It was her regular practise to exercise this habit whenever the opportunity presented itself and many were the moments when she would take the opportunity to exercise this fancy of hers for her own surreal pleasure: The children soon learned from bitter experience, that there was always a need to exercise a particular caution when clowning around among themselves: (a careful eye always being trained towards the door!) The possibility always existing that the chance of discovery might not be too far away and if anyone did happen to appear, it would certainly be without anything approaching a prior warning; appearing suddenly like a spectral ghost, upon the scene: It often happened that we would be engaged in careless horseplay; absorbed in our game: We would consequently have been unaware of the spectre that emerged suddenly from behind a doorway: Silently would she walk into the room that we were playing in, creeping with an unbridled enthusiasm, towards our direction, rolling up her sleeve as she moved with her look of unqualified anticipation: She then raised her arm with an exaggerated venom and struck the unsuspecting boy, as hard as she could, across his ear: He was the unfortunate one that had had his back to her: Her practiced art was evident in the speed of the attack; a skill at which she was undoubtedly adept: The attack was always exercised with the venom of a dedicated assault charge, so that any attempt at diminishing the ferocity of the blow would only be alleviated by detecting the speed and direction of the blow with sufficient time: All that the rest of us could do was to stand by and observe the whole proceeding with a helpless futility, whenever it was that these attacks took place, perhaps thanking our lucky stars that at least it hadn't been our turn this time. The enjoyment and the malice that she achieved from these victories were in themselves their own dreadful culture shock, and the pleasure that she displayed at the successful attainment of these assaults, as she strode away with a look of triumph and achievement, meant only that the whole scenario was made more obscene and painful for the rest of us: The only thing left for us to do was only to stand idly by and watch with helpless impotency as the futility and repugnancy of the whole scenario left us all feeling helpless and alone.

Notwithstanding the levels of confusion that close personal familiarity engendered among all of the children, the levels of understanding and the prevailing affinity within all of the children, meant that a tacit appreciation of the relationship between us all was always mutually understood, preventing outright expressions of physical and verbal abuse and otherwise excessive behaviour, from being rendered as unacceptable tenets of social conviction, within the group of children as a whole.

I cannot let this matter pass at this point without the mention of a condition that persisted on a regular basis in the home, due to that same misguided diligence relating to some of the nuns and also because of the practices of some of the older boys as well: The names of the nuns and the boys have been burned into my memory and that, sadly is where they have to remain: I can offer no good service to any of these people by attempting to resurrect the names of otherwise miscreant practitioners who chose, in this infertile atmosphere, to exercise a tendency to inflict pain and punishment on any unfortunate weaker beings. The incidence of bullying and mistreatment in the home was perpetrated continuously with an avid zeal, leading to the generally subliminal malaise of fear and a subsequent reaction that often became endemic, particularly insofar as the younger children were concerned: They usually exercised a defensive responses to attacks by raising their arms above their heads, so as to deflect any blows that were being directed towards them: Something of an insignificance, you might suppose, when related to the patterns of behaviour that involved this tendency towards personal protection: When any potential threat is directed against another boy, they will already have developed these levels of mistrust and any lack of confidence in themselves, in the first place: The abiding consequence of this situation is the reticence of any real affinity towards their fellows, verging almost on an incoherent social distrust, not because children learn at an early age about the need to preserve these elements of secrecy about shared relationships, but because the people who are in control are so adept and skilful at the distribution of torment and division, particularly when it pleases them to play one child against another, most of the time.

I can reasonably claim therefore, that as a general rule, we were inclined to keep pretty much to ourselves, during most of our time together, if only to maintain a personal degree of privacy, insofar as any kind of relationship might exist with people 'outside' rather than within the home, and it did usually ensure all of us a rare kind of camaraderie between ourselves that also encouraged that same instinctive need for self-preservation from any other emotional predators that were never very far away: Conversely, and as a consequence of this contradictory relationship quandary, as a group together, we would usually all be united as thickly as thieves might have been, whenever a moment came along that involved any threats to the security of the group as a whole.

As already mentioned, a prevailing aspect of the brutality that was manifested in the treatment of many of the children was the impulsive mannerism that had evolved of its own accord, among the children in the home: The intention always remained the same, of raising arms in self-defence or of simply deflecting a blow, whether the threat was being delivered by one of the older boys or by one of the nuns: The fact that was most chilling about these actions was the reliance by the children on these immediate impulse responses, even if the threat was not actually being presented at all, at that moment: In its simplest form, of course we all referred to this action as 'flinching' but it was a reaction that became almost as intuitive as any automatic response to any form of danger: A defensive mechanism, to be sure, but one that was always effective when applied as a countermeasure reaction as well.

The Chapel; the integral point of the whole convent structure remained as the spiritual and emotional heart of any and all religious activity at Nazareth house. Apart from the usual church services every day, mass and benediction, there were allways regular visits to the chapel, made both by the nuns and by the children, for the purpose of celebrating various saint's days, as well as the feasts of Advent and Lent: On religious feast days, we were required to attend at church, and on many of those days, we would often be required to sing masses as well. Many other religious events also occurred on a regular basis, particularly during Advent and Lent, that were the moments in the year that were as much devoted to the dedication of prayer as were the celebrations of various other feast days, of which there were many in the Christian calendar: They involved regular marches by the children, into the pews reserved for the children. The chapel served as the focal point of all worship for many Christian feasts and we spent prolonged periods of our time on our knees in prayerful introspection. We were always involved, to some degree in all of the religious activities in the church and if we were not actually present at a service, we would still be involved in making preparations for them, unless we were actually working in our classroom. at the time

Regular church services, attended by the children, usually meant Mass and Benediction, always on Sundays but on other feast days as well, that happened on a regular basis throughout the year and certainly on nominated feasts or 'holy' days': The nuns always sat together, separated from the general public and the children, in their own section of the church; a portion of the Church located to one side of the altar, where we were not able to see them, but neither were they able to keep their eye on us either; a mildly comforting arrangement, to our way of thinking, as it meant that it was one of the more satisfying moments when, at least for a while, we were not being regarded for their attention.

The children provided the choir for all of the services, when they were required to do so, in the church. The choir always remained a prominent feature of the service as the provider of its musical propriety, insofar as it was invariably represented to support church services whenever it was required: These services usually took place at least once a week, and the service of benediction took place as well, but not on such a regular basis, and always in the evening.

That is not to say that the children attended morning mass on every day of the week, but usually only on Sundays and feast days: There were certainly exceptions to this rigid arrangement because there were always events in the Christian calendar that meant further religious obeisance needed to be observed: Different church services also took place on special feast days and these occurred between the regular ones that always ran on, throughout the year. The reader must divine all that he wishes to understand, from the careful suggestions that I am attempting to impart, of the compliant impact that daily life, the church and religion, held on all of our daily lives. The power of prayer was absorbed into our very consciousness through the insistent repetition of these religious concepts, that have probably continued unchanged since the beginning of time.

There was one event in the Christian calendar that occurred in a four-week period each year and was an arrangement that involved all of the residents in the convent, both the nuns and the children in an exercise of prayer and a rigidly maintained silence throughout the day. We were required not even to talk to each other for the whole period of the session. The activity in question was called a 'retreat' and it involved regular daily visits to the church to receive our religious instruction from a 'white father' (a special kind of monk) that stayed at the home for the duration of the retreat. We all engaged religiously in our prayers during this period and 'fasted' which meant actually dispensing with one kind of food every day. We adhered diligently to the fabric of this retreat, absorbing with enthusiasm the concept of religious fervour that this whole exercise involved

As I mentioned before, one of the important acquisitions, prided by many of the older boys was the obtaining of books, known as 'missals' (special prayer books!) into which were included pictures of saints and other holy images, all added for additional embellishment: Prayer constituted much of the input and perception that became so much a part of our lives and we whole heartedly acknowledged the whole concept of pious integration with the rabid enthusiasm of a dried and empty sponge.

On the whole we were considered to be rather good at our singing and people from the local area would travel some distance to enjoy the choir (or so we were told!). The fame of the choir, certainly at a local level, meant that the church was always full if a mass or other service was going to be sung and especially during Christmas night or the Easter services. Time was allotted on every Sunday morning for choir practice, where nervous energy might be better expended, in the practice of tone scales and such, often also singing a full mass, from the beginning to the end, until the session finally ended. Memorabilia actually circulated among the boys, relating to the 'Festival of Britain' event, that had been presented to some boys that had performed there, at that time, and in which some of the Nazareth house boys had actually been involved: 1951 was sadly, too long before my time, so that while choir practice was still a regular event on Sundays, and one that was not normally to be missed, we were, as a matter of course, always regularly employed accompanying church services all of the time while we lived in the convent.

Religious involvement and the rigorous climate that was Roman Catholicism, was the only one that existed or was tolerated by the nuns, within the confines of the home, and the only one that existed as a cornerstone of Christian belief structure: The sisters diligently observed it with an abiding sincerity and an emotional ardour, generated by the overriding proximity of religion, all of the time, exuding its exorbitant zeal even among the more unwilling of the children: It expressed itself ultimately in passionate expressions of religious piety, evolving itself ultimately in an enthusiasm towards the faith, that children, as a whole were happy to integrate with and to absorb with a new found naivety: It might not have been so easy to discourage these rampant tendencies, even if one had had the temerity within themselves, to attempt such efforts: Perish the thought that such a thing might even have been considered as a possibility in any event, since the whole question of religion was introduced initially, with much deliberation and purpose, from a very early stage in a child's life.

At one point, during my stay at the house, I even gave serious consideration to applying to join the priesthood in the catholic church: I applied for and was accepted, to be enrolled into the church's own training college at Campion House, a Catholic priest training seminar, in London; I even practiced and became passably good at learning the basics of the Latin language, in preparation for what I had hoped would be the beginnings of my new vocational voyage: It was however fortunate for me that I was soon redirected from this particular path, persuaded instead by the more sensible notion that I was perhaps not heading down the most sensible of roads in my attempt at pursuing more positive future goals, even with such wholly impractical options incorporated. The most sensible reason proposed at the time was that the consequences of a serious lack of life experience and a possible inability to cope with ongoing life issues that I might have encountered in the future, was not really going to help me in my quest, of actually coming to terms with any of the justifications for this sensible advice, in the first place: I did resent what I felt was an unreasonable intrusion into aspirations that I had nurtured, for my future personal development plans: With the ongoing passage of time however, I am grateful now, for that gentle wisdom, as hindsight has been kinder to me than the naivety that existed within me, at that time, might have allowed me to be, and I dread to think of the turn that this ramshackle life might have taken, had I continued to pursue that particular goal: I am grateful today for the timely intervention of wiser heads, at a time when it was of greater importance to me.

The first action of every day and also the last one of every night was the reciting of daily prayers. This function was almost an automatic one, involving the waking up of children in the morning, first thing, whereupon I would instantly leap from my bed, in an automated fashion; to kneel down and proceed to recite my morning prayers: This process was always performed in precisely the same manner in the evening, except that on those occasions we all knelt together and prayed before an appointed effigy, with our hands joined together in prayerful supplication, reciting prayers in the same orderly fashion: Just one more consequence of a repetitive behaviour syndrome.

An engagement that none of the boys ever objected getting involved with was the task of serving at the altar, assisting the priest while he was engaged in leading the church service, whether it was at Mass or Benediction: it was a prized opportunity that we were allowed to perform for a whole week: It did mean that we enjoyed a substantial elevation of status: We were able to bask in that task, knowing that, while it might only have been for a short time, we were at least raised to a level that made us feel just that bit more superior than the rest of the children: Serving at the altar during the church service was a function that the older boys were usually required to perform every day, for a week at a time: The two boys that were chosen to serve were expected to rise early in the morning, earlier even than the rest of the children, as mass always began rather early in the day, and then to make themselves available in an adjoining room in the church, called the vestry (the altar boys changing room.) where we got robed up in appropriate cassocks and attended to the serving of the priest as he performed at the altar: We were obviously quite happy to participate in these tasks, if only because it elevated us to a higher degree of stature among the other children, and because it enabled also us to avoid some of the tasks that were waiting to be attended to by the other, more unfortunate children, after they had all eaten their breakfast.

One young priest visited us regularly around this time: His name was Father David Chapman: We particularly liked him because he appeared to be a kinder sort of person but also because he was friendly with the boys in the nicest possible way, even sharing the odd joke or humorous aside while he waited with us, to enter the altar: We were certainly more at ease in his company than we had been with any of the other priests, a fact that resulted in no small but tangible resentment from watching nuns: (nobody ever laughed or played in their church!) He was like a breath of fresh air in the starchy climate of our restrictive confines and we all thought the world of him: He even owned a motor cycle, a Triumph Bonneville, that he often arrived at the house on, riding it in through the gates; a fact that, in our eyes, elevated him almost to the level of Godhead: It must have been at about this same time that I discovered an article that had been written about him in a magazine called 'MOTORCYCLE NEWS' that was a popular motor cycling magazine, at that time, in which he was introduced with some fanfare to its front page with the titled heading of 'Ton up Chaplain'. I only know that he was the most delightfully charming proponent of the Catholic faith that I ever had the pleasure of meeting.

The practice of burning charcoal in the chasuble (The vessel that distributed the smoke and the scent of the incense throughout the church) meant that when it was placed on top of the burning coals, it released a stream of smoke directly into the nostrils: Imagine my surprise then, when we were called into the sacristy (the room that the serving priest used to prepare for the service, before we accompanied him to the altar) Father Chapman had taken the chasuble from me on this particular occasion and proceeded to swing it around, above his head, from the floor up to the ceiling, in a swinging circular motion, several times, at considerable speed, to our amazement and delight: I always understood the importance of the practice anyway, since it was essential to ensure that air was provided at all times, around the charcoal that was burning inside, to ensure that it was always kept hot: For ourselves however, it remained sufficient to the moment that we continue to keep it swinging as we entered the altar to proceed with the service. To boys however who had never seen anything like this before, it was like a breath of fresh air, a momentary diversion wherein we actually felt that we were being allowed into one small part of an informal local rebellion: He was such a laid-back man and such a refreshing revelation of what good people might actually have been like, in some other world: Sadly, as far as I was aware, there were too few of his kind, that actually alighted on this planet; I won't soon forget you for that! Dear Father Chapman!

I should add in passing that I have never lost a fondness for the infectious smell of incense and I still enjoy the porous odour that emanates from joss sticks when I am still able to use them these days, at home.

Serving at the altar was a familiarly mundane function in its way, providing the priest with the water and the wine as it was required, and performing other necessary procedures that enabled a service to run its course with dutiful efficiency: With a familiarity that came with repetition, we were soon able to attend to the needs of the priest with a comforting consistency. It also meant, of course that we were also able to avoid the more pressing and menial tasks that were always required to be completed after the children had had their breakfast.

At around nine or ten of their years all of the children were given an opportunity to take the Sacrament (The first Holy Communion) arranged as a special Sunday celebration: All the children were dressed in splendid new clothes, of all white colour, and they all looked agreeably resplendent in their new outfits: All of the children that were receiving their first communion paraded together on the lawn at the front of the house. This was a very special day that included a specially prepared breakfast and a plentiful supply of gushing congratulation, and then there was all of the fuss and all of the praise: Dressed in fine clothes, the children all looked resplendent as they displayed themselves to a host of admiring accolades. Sadly, the elevation to this new and more delightful level of personal fantasy did not last for too long, as the harsh reality that was always the legacy of normal life in the home, soon engaged with them again together with a related disenchantment that ensued with the sad end to that heavenly day. It was certainly the best of times for all of the new Holy communicants and it was certainly one that they would have had good reason to remember for the rest of their lives: The attainment of this privilege however involved them in their having to learn and to be fully conversant with the catechism (the small book that contained all of the basic diktats of Roman Catholicism) by heart, before qualifying for the privileges and rewards that they would have attained, once they had received the sacrament: It did mean however, by the same token, that they would then be able to receive the host at mass: (The body of Christ:) providing they had not sinned or otherwise erred in the meantime; however a visit to the local ' confessional ' to absolve oneself of outstanding sins or misdemeanours before hand, usually resolved that little issue anyway, since absolution was always granted in the confessional, with any other sins purged from those erring souls at the same time, as a consequence! I myself was not permitted to take my first holy communion with the other children, not because I was in anyway remiss with my catechism studies but because of the course of events that my life took, in a manner that I will discuss in more detail later, coming into effect to prevent it all from actually happening.

CHAPTER 4

Education

W hile I have touched lightly on this formative period of my learning life and the fact that I am able to remember only the more comforting moments of that time, when I was in infant school, I do remember that I enjoyed hearing and reading stories, particular on topics relating to English language subjects; stories and such: I recall the fact that while the subject of reading was usually met with loud protestations, the other children were never very comfortable with that idea anyway: I probably smiled a little to myself, inwardly, always insisting to the teacher that I would rather read or be read to, and hoping that she would agree with me when we were all asked, whatever it was that we wanted to do next: Perhaps she enjoyed the reading aspects of these lessons, as well!

I have no meaningful recollections of this particular period of my life, prior to my move to a higher age group, in the house: Needless to say, it did remain a point in my life that still remained as mostly a mental blank, which is why perhaps, I have opted to embellish it instead, if only mildly, with a few anecdotes that might pass for inconsequential baggage in the overall context that is this whole sorry tale: I have chosen not to dwell on any of the consequences that might have related to events for which there might have been ramifications for the overall life structure of this tale: All I can hold on to after all of this, are the speculations and suspicions relating to any possible unreasonable treatment that might have occurred as a consequence of matters that are now sadly beyond my recollection: There are no opportunities for adequate memory recovery, so that all that I can reasonably suppose is that repercussions caused by actions that might have been taken at this time, still continue to plague all of my daily functions and all of my daily comforts, even to this very day.

I was transferred to the main children's area from the infant's section at 'Nazareth house', Southend, at the age of seven years. It is now, 1953; the year of the queen's coronation. The only detail that I can recall about that time is the preponderance of 'Union Jacks' that decked every building as far as the eye could see: The whole town was ablaze with them.

The school classroom at Nazareth house was of a reasonable size, sufficient necessarily that it could accommodate about thirty children: The desks were positioned in three rows, placed down the left, right and centre of the room: A large desk, for the teacher; was positioned at the front of the classroom. I began what I still consider to be the start of my formal education in this same classroom, partly because this was the moment in my life that I am most able to remember with a reasonable degree of accuracy: In what I had always thought of as being the big boys school, l can still recall an overwhelming feeling of excitement and anticipation at the prospect that was being presented to me with this new lifetime opportunity: I still recall the enthusiasm that I felt when I first arrived in that classroom: We all began our first day by being seated at our allocated desks, lined up in what became forever more our own individual places: All of the children, myself included, were issued with what we had thought of as being fine new writing implements, but were in fact rather more loose leaf affairs, jotting pads, pens and the like, all, in actual fact, of doubtful and durable quality and probably ones that would only have passed muster if they had actually been employed for the purpose of jotting down notes and for any other summary part time uses: I recall thinking at the time how much of a wonderful and novel event this whole new school experience thing was turning out to be for me, and how much I approaching this whole new education experience with a singular degree of optimism and anticipation; (at least at the beginning.)

a sad fact of life, on the face of it, that became increasingly less engaging with the illuminating passage of time: In fact it was not too long before the whole new school excitement moment degenerated into a more pragmatic form of resigned disillusionment The children in the class were all issued with a selection of writing materials; pens, rubbers and rulers,(but unfortunately not with blotting paper!) an essential addition as it happened, essential in alleviating any problems or oversights that might have occur in the processing of the work, and including the statutory ink in the containers, provided for the purpose, in receptacles in the desks: Insignificant considerations in themselves, you might suppose, but to the uninitiated eye, the engendered promise of a bright new start in what was potentially a new and promising future: These items, rudimentary in their own way, as opposed to what are considered 'today' as modern day accoutrements, were all available in the classrooms of the time, existing as the more inefficient implements of their day, without either benefit or foreknowledge of any future difficulty that might yet have accrued by the attainment of their successful use, and which might also have been gained from their regular application, either: Modern day students might be tempted to think that this is an image portrayed as the most wonderful of new beginnings for all of us, and we certainly viewed our future educational prospects with an unbridled enthusiasm, at the time: The classroom was a normal one, of large and nondescript appearance and size: When you've seen one of these old fashioned class rooms, then you've probably seen them all: The lines of desks ran down the centre of the room with the largest one, for the teacher placed right at the front, commanding the whole area and dominating the classroom, occupied by the teacher: Also positioned at the front of the room stood a grand piano, although I don't ever recall it ever was used for all of the time that I actually stayed there.

For our ill fortune, we were 'gifted' with a teacher who we soon discovered was perhaps the most contentious of people ever to be imposed on a group of children: That was certainly how it appeared to be, to us, in very short order: As far as any relationship between the teacher and his pupils was concerned, it became primarily the most unsettling of mutual interactions that it could ever have been possible to imagine: It appeared indeed that the storyline for this particular person should have read more like the script from some vague Dickensian novel; rather more a narrative tale of robust education practice that exceeded the bounds of what was considered acceptable educational procedure, certainly at this time: I regret to tell you that all of my perceptions of this teacher will have to remain in the negative, since, as difficult as it remains for me to personify, this whole tale will remain as true reality: Any positive attributes have been carefully defined and remain as unembellished ingredients in the details of this story: I am unable to recall any aspect of his demeanour as being anything rather than angry and aggressive. While I will obviously attempt to include any positive aspects of such a variable personality into the details that relate to him, nothing of an amicable persuasion has come readily to mind. It would be unreasonable I suppose to assume that he might possibly have been an entirely unfriendly and unaffable person, unless perhaps while he was in some other place, socialising with his close associates; out of hours: It is more than I can believe that he might have lived a whole life, coping with the contentious and contradictory outlook that he consistently displayed in the classroom: I can only assume that the anger and the mood swings to which we were constantly subjected, may have been due to changes that were evident in his personal condition and possibly due also to a less than healthy lifestyle: It is difficult to offer an opinion that will prove to be accurate and unqualified, about the man, considering the fact of his advancing years as well, for he was undoubtedly not a young person: He spent most of his day in the classroom, seated at his desk, chewing repeatedly on RENNIE tablets that were always placed comfortably within his coat pocket: It is therefore reasonable to assume that he suffered substantially from what appeared to have been a recurring gastric condition: Seated at his desk, he seemed content just to sit and glare at his class, casting a baleful eye over a tremulous, apprehensive flock, perhaps deciding in which direction he might next vent his spleen, and the direction of the unfortunate miscreant. It was not surprising, therefore that, for the majority of the time that we were in his attendance, attempting to imbibe ourselves of his educational imperatives, we were subjected, as a matter of course, to his customary tirades of intimidation and aggression: We all lived in fear of him and it was a careless child that had the temerity to spoil a writing book during his attempts at transcribing dictation onto the page, particularly with the questionable assistance of singularly unsuitable writing materials: He appeared to enjoy the dictation sessions, when he was able to proceed, by reciting a section of some book or other to the class, pacing up and down between the lines of desks as he did so, waiting only to administer his retribution to any child careless enough to make a mess of his work. Care had to be taken not to use too much ink on the nib as it invariably left blots of ink on the paper; and just as regrettably, blotting paper, treasured and retained by the more fortunate, was the one item that most of us could only dream of owning. We all lived in terror of him as he prowled between the desks, armed with what he liked to think of as his pudding stick, ready with a snarl, to inflict his anger on any child foolish enough to irritate an already uncertain demeanour. He was certainly attached to that stick, clearly his first weapon of choice, as he never seemed to miss an opportunity to use it to best effect against any of us: He liked mostly, to use the stick on body parts that were exposed to his line of sight, on the top of the desk; hands, fingers or even regular limbs that remained in view: He might alternatively throw it, with unusually determinate accuracy, from a position behind his desk: The outcome, generally speaking, was usually the same and just as generally, resulted in the same final outcome.

One practice that was regularly employed in the classroom was his preferred punishment, that he liked to refer to as 'drilling': This activity was required to be performed by one or more of the children on most days during the week. It was normally inflicted on any child who had irritated him in one way or another: This drilling punishment involved the penitent child sitting on the floor behind the piano at the front of the class with his arms folded across his chest. He was then required to stand up and then sit down, repeatedly; standing up and sitting down, but with the arms remaining folded across the chest, throughout the exercise, until the teacher would finally remembered to return the boy to his seat, some time later on.

He wore the same large brown coat that always seemed to be too heavy for him to carry on his shoulders, and when he walked, he bore with him what appeared to me to be a permanent limp and an accompanying stoop, perhaps caused by the infliction of his original condition, of which I was singularly unaware. I have a lasting memory that I still hold of him, that involves me with a little dismay as I watched him walk along with what seemed to me to be a permanently debilitating gait: It appeared to me that he was just about able to get along with little of reasonable comfort, tending a bad leg with each step that he took.

His demeanour in the classroom always deteriorated rapidly, as the day wore on and the consequences of any personal difficulties that he might have been nursing at the time drove him into bouts of an uncontrollable rage: He could display the foulest of tempers and bared his teeth at us in continual displays of uncontrollable rage, but just as possibly as an expression of a real pain expression, which meant that an unpleasant demeanour, already festering as the day wore on, only grew more intense with the passage of time: We were all in total fear of him and he was certainly not above expressing his unbridled irritation towards boys when the mood took him, to the extent that he consistently prowled through the class while we bent to our tasks, transcribing dictation or engaging in any other kind of schoolwork that he demanded from us, leading usually to persistent acts of petulance towards any unfortunate boy who failed to perform a particular task to his satisfaction. It wasn't so much that he struck boys around the head, which he did all the time with as much enthusiasm as he was capable of, as it was the abusive verbal lashings at cowed boys heads, invariably accompanied by physical punishments, that occurred at the same time.

This is just a brief description of the period of time that was spent in the attendance of this teacher: It is in no way intended to be presented as a statement that bears any unqualified animosity towards him by any the boys, or even by this writer: He was dedicated to the education of 'his' boys, in his own inimitable way and he had been teaching at the school for more years than I could possibly have known about and had probably always been comfortable with an education culture that had been an acceptable one during earlier periods of his working life but which did not perhaps sit so comfortably with the new social changes to his culture regime, that had been coming increasingly into play: Probably indeed, for as long as the house was operated as a care home by the nuns: He had after all laboured continually throughout what must have been severe pain levels, and if that degree of encumbrance had indeed included constant expressions of anger, in whatever direction it might have suited him to direct it, in his more painful moments of emotional intent, then that was a cross that the children in his care were destined to carry, for the remainder of his working life.

Much of the school work that we were engaged with was expressed as dictation that we all disliked intensely: It involved the kind of persuasive stimulus and encouragement culture that expressed itself in various kinds of physical persuasion. The exercises involved transcribing written words, dictated by him as he paced up and down between the aisles, on to our books, as the words were read out to us, as quickly and as precisely as we were able to transcribe them: We were also required to complete the work as quickly and as carefully as possible: The exercise of writing down words on to paper was obviously considered to be important and it was one that we were usually required to undertake in at least one period of class every day: Not the easiest of tasks, I can promise you, with an inkpot full of ink and a scratchy, makeshift pen that was required to be dipped constantly into a pot, then carefully employed, without making too much of a mess, on to paper: We were always consciously aware of the patrolling menace looming over us all of the time while he dictated, armed with a heavy hand and the inevitable pudding stick, waiting to beat at the bowed heads of recalcitrant children who had taken too long a time in completing the exercise: It did not seem to me that we actually engaged with too many of the more important subjects I felt could perhaps have been more readily included in this otherwise questionable curriculum: Reading, certainly but I don't recall too much of anything else. To be fair there must have been other activities that would have engaged us at the school but I really have no memory of any of them and I cannot recall anything constructive ever being achieved in terms of any of the subjects that were taught to us during our stay at Nazareth house that might have involved our abilities, in any way, to adjust to the higher standards that might be required, had I ever moved to a different school and actually needed those supporting skills to help me engage with a new school curriculum: All of the lessons that were applied at Nazareth house were all confined to a single classroom and there was never an occasion when we engaged in an activity that might have taken place outside of those four walls: The possibility of taking part in any kind of educational activity that would actually have taken us beyond that classroom and allowed the children some respite from the rigours of a more formal kind of education, that we were all familiar with anyway, was never likely to come to fruition: Indeed, any shortcomings in my education would probably have been highlighted when I moved at a later stage into a different school; but more of that later! Misdemeanours, however trivial were sufficient to drive this man into an incoherent rage: We never dared to laugh out of turn or even to venture a glance in his direction: He considered even visual acquiescence to be on the same level as a personal affront: Who are you looking at, boy", followed by inevitable recriminations.

The application of punishment, it appeared was an activity that was practiced with a considerable amount of enthusiasm by all of the established authority figures at Nazareth house: The teacher, first and foremost but also the senior boys and of course, some of the nuns as well. It appears to have been the glue that cemented this whole concept of culture control together, into one cohesive principle that guaranteed the assured level of conditional subservience: I recall for instance several occasions during the time that I spent at the school when I was punished for various misdemeanours, which reason I can't even recall now; but I can certainly recall what the outcome of those punishments were: For some odd reason these punishments always repeated themselves on Fridays; the same day that excessively greasy fish lunches were served up to the children, and I would just as contentedly eat mine as well: Unfortunately, the coincidence of two apparently disconnected events caused what became the coordination of two unsolicited outcomes to arrive at an eventual and unfortunate fruition: I was not prepared for instance, for the added ministration of punishment on this same Friday afternoon. The punishment required that I kneel on the floor at the front of the class, in an upright position with my hands folded behind my back and my head held upright, there I was to remain for an indeterminate time: As I said, nothing had prepared me for an afternoon of additional penance and for the sequence of events that followed it: Having succeeded in upsetting the teacher, how, I do not recall, I found that I was unable to maintain that position for long as the combination of greasy fish and uncompromising punishment regime meant that the whole situation became more difficult for me to maintain than I could reasonably deal with: Eventually, I became violently sick and nauseous: The outcome of this particular episode was the admission of my condition (a rare event on its own!) and the exclusion from the class for the rest of the day. This episode actually repeated itself on a second occasion, oddly enough, almost on the chronological same day. This event was actually repeated on a subsequent Friday and also in the afternoon and also involving a stomach full of greasy fish again (we always ate fish on Fridays!) I dislike relating facts that seem almost too implausible to be real but I can only offer this truth as an object of absolute faith and hope that it will be accepted as such by any reader of this tale.

The teacher at Nazareth house comfortably endorsed the practice of 'drilling' on a regular basis as another of his own practical educational aids and the most convenient form of disciplinary ministration that was available to him. How it was that he had first decided on the advantages of this kind of discipline in the first place, and for how long it had actually continued, I will never know: All that I am sure about is that it was a practice that began earlier than I can remember, when I first arrived at the school and it had been applied without pause as the standard tool of admonishment for all of the time that I was staying there. This activity did however provide for some issues of its own: The only space that was available for this drilling, that was appropriate to the purpose was the most convenient one between the piano and the front wall of the room, which meant that the boys had to exercise, across the floor, in a single line: There was, as a result, always one unfortunate child, positioned on the outside of the line who would be the one seated closest to the teacher and directly across from his desk. As a result, he would be the one, best placed as he was, to be positioned at the end of the line, and in the way that children are inclined to behave when left on their own, it would not have been too long before some kind of distraction caused us all to pause as one, in our penal endeavours until a well-directed stick and a snarl would fly directly in the direction of the boys, usually with considerable accuracy. "Get on with it!" would be the angry shout as we leapt once more into our renewed and terrified activity. The thing that he insisted on calling his pudding stick remained as the disparaging description of an item that while small, sharp and heavy, was capable of carrying the real promise of physical damage, had his aim been more accurate.

I can only suppose, because of his failing health, that he was perhaps entitled to be a bit cranky: I can only assume that by this time, he will have moved on, bless him; but I will always understand that in his own way he cared a great deal for the boys: He had taught them all for such a long time: the school must really have been the one fixture of his life purpose; he had worked there for so many years, by all accounts and was certainly dedicated to the work to which he had been able to express so much of his enthusiasm and encouragement for his boys, again in his own inimitable manner: We all left that school eventually, to go to our different and alternative ones, placed outside the home, soon afterwards anyway and so I suppose that grudgingly, he finally went off on his own way as well.

I used to wonder whether the combination of a delicate constitution and regular visits to the 'Cricketers arms' were really conducive to this teacher's continuing poor health but of course it was something that we would never have considered talking about openly, even among ourselves.

In 1957 at age eleven, a new liberalism was infecting many of the old and aging aspects that had been a fact of convent life up to that time: Arrangements had already been made to transfer the children from the convent school to a different, alternative one, located beyond its normal sphere of influence and its perimeter: The first one was a local catholic school; St. Helen's RC primary school, where life became just a shade more acceptable, if only because the journey to the new school now involved a ten minute walk along a main road, outside of the convent, indicating to me the prospect of a new and revised liberty scenario: The classes were still held together in a single large room and we still seemed to enjoy much the same educational prospect; having only one teacher for all of the classes and one classroom to learn all of the lessons in, but at least the range of subjects that were on offer did improve slightly and I did enjoy a pleasant, if still slightly limited learning experience for the next two years.

Sadly, what did not change noticeably was the same insistence on implementing corporal punishment practice into that school's disciplinary code: It was not so much overt or abusive to be sure but it still persisted with the same degree of uncontrolled enthusiasm; the kind that I had believed I had actually left behind me, when I finally left the one in the convent.

I cannot pretend that I was a clever and studious student: I'm afraid that I opted to sit at the back of the class and I was also inclined to play around somewhat and disrupt things when I should perhaps have been more focussed on my schoolwork: There were occasions indeed when I was called to the front of the class by the teacher to receive his retribution: He had, for this task a thick ruler that he kept in his desk, for the sole purpose of administering punishment: It had a steel edge incorporated into it, that he probably found most expedient to his purpose of inflicting the greatest degree of pain that he was potentially capable of doing, to my outstretched hand: I could only watch as he raised the stick with a determination and an energy that he was able to comfortably express in the speed and direction of his ultra-tutorial, but misguided skills. For my part, I was content just to regard it all as the extension of a practice that, for me had always been just one more bane of a daily life existence: I had so become adjusted, a long time ago, to punishments, administered, usually as a matter of course, that I was probably well inured of the whole retribution concept, anyway: Come to think of it, I actually wonder whether this teacher might actually have gained for himself a similar degree of comfort from the activity, at the same time that he was engaged in visiting it on me.

The year is now 1959 and I have now arrived at the tender age of 13 years: I moved finally to a new school that had just been completed, also in Southend: St. Thomas More High school: Surprisingly, I was actually appointed to become a school prefect in that school: (No! I never became accustomed to that whole prefect thing either!) I was chosen to perform this duty with commendable diligence, but never did I do it with any of the relish that I was perhaps required to employ in the performance of the duty: It would never have been my purpose to wilfully enforce discipline of any kind, nor did the responsibility that it involved me in, of expressing any of those disciplines, ever rest heavily on my shoulders: I can only deduce that harder hearts than mine were, might have been sufficiently strong that they could achieve the kind of success required for the effective functioning of disciplinary enforcement and I can never really recall ever settling into that task in a meaningful way: I can only assume that, purely on a personal level, I probably lacked the inclination to dominate at any level, simply for its own sake: Just so has it always been and just so will it probably always remain: This at least, is an aspect of my life that has now finally ended: The continuing incidence of personal abuse that had always dominated my life has now finally finished, as are all of the controls that might have been incorporated, relating to the forms of bullying and intimidation that had always blighted my life: The old days of threats and punishment have now been consigned finally, to the waste bin thankfully, of discarded old memories and I can only thank God that the imperial entity that was previous school history is no longer a part of my life's culture any more: From now on, I will try to continue with what remains of my head and my heart, and my new life and I can hope also that things work out in my favour, in any future that I am destined to inherit at this new school.

For our arrival at the new school; 'St Thomas More high school', we were all clothed in smart new maroon uniforms and provided with smart new clothes: We were even driven to the new school, about two miles away, each day in a minibus: I recall being instructed, at the time of our arrival at the school only to give our home address, when asked, as 111, London road rather than as Nazareth house: It was never that much of a matter of concern for any of the boys, as we were all content to answer any questions about where we all lived anyway, if we were ever questioned, on the matter.

It was a nice school, I suppose: Fine and new and it felt so alive and full of ambition and promise; oodles of optimism and of course, my bright new future: Sadly, all it really did for me was to highlight many of my own shortcomings and my limitations, insofar as vocational abilities were concerned: In all of my new curricular subjects I found myself lacking in the required standards of education, probably perceived of as being basic skill levels, relating to what should have been achievable for a child of my age: In mathematics I had no perception or understanding of either algebra or trigonometry, having never been introduced to any of these subjects at any time in my life: That same failing, I discovered, applied to almost the whole range of subjects that were available to me at the school, as part of this new school syllabus. The only real fact of importance that I soon learned to appreciate was the realisation of what effect the lack of any suitable basic education was going to have on what had always been a numbingly narrow educational curriculum level during past school years. Most of the early school learning that I had been ever been subjected to, up to that moment in time had all been sustained in the name of an education system that had always constituted most of my young life's upbringing up to that moment: I could not claim to have any knowledge or understanding of any of the new disciplines that involved modern education structure and I discovered that most of the subjects that I was required to deal with in this new school were as vague to me as a new foreign language might have been: The saddest fact of all in all of this sorry history of sad facts is that the specialist teachers whom I had believed would be the ones most involved from now on, with the intellectual development of new students, while claiming professional titles for themselves, relating to subjects in which they claimed to have specialist knowledge, seemed not to have had any particular interest, at the end of the day in their primary function of dedicating themselves to the personal and mental development of their students, and of me in particular: Personally, both as a student and also as a human being. I was unable to regard any future prospects that might have included, achieving any gainful relevance in this new future that I was now confronted with, with a great deal of confidence, based on the premise that I was attempting to engage with, at this time, in this new school!

In the initial stages, I was quite taken with the concept of different classes for different subjects; a new and novel experience for me, and a brand new headmaster to boot, as well; Harold Wilson Curry: He rather took me under his wing at the new school and introduced me to many aspects of history and the arts that represented a whole new learning experience for me: Perhaps he saw things in me that I had never had the opportunity to discover for myself: I discovered that he existed as the contradiction of all of my existing perceptions about what I had believed to be the general standard of attainment in my new teachers: I have certainly never looked back on the encouragement that he provided for me when he took me under his wing.

The teachers at the school, bless them were unwilling to a man to cater to my faltering abilities and were by the same token, deficient in their own levels of patience and tolerance. So much for all of my promising new hopes and all of those wonderful multi room classes! I had considered my experience in this new school to be the beginning of a wonderful new educational genesis, but sadly, when I did finally leave the school, it was with rather more a downcast feeling of disenchantment and disillusionment.

On mealtimes

The part of the house in which we all shared our meals was called the refectory: It was a singularly large space that accommodated sufficient tables for all of the children to be seated, all in one sitting, in the house, to eat all of the meals together: It had a functional layout that addressed the requirement of simple organised control, with sufficient tables around the room, seating five children each, plus a senior boy who always sat at the end of the table. One boy at the table was given the job of taking the empty teapot over to the tea urn, positioned at the entrance to the refectory, at the beginning of each meal, so that it might be filled up and returned to the table: It would then be quickly poured out into cups so that the emptied teapot could be quickly returned once more to the urn to be topped up again, one more time, before the meal finally commenced: Urgency in this matter was essential as it ensured that there would be sufficient tea for everyone to be able to enjoy a second cup: There was never sufficient tea in the urn to enable it to go all the way around again so that expediency in this matter was always the order of the day: One had always to be careful about such things: On the strength of details such as this, did the amicability of a contented table continue to depend.

After grace, (a prayer that we all recited before our meals.) a practice that we always observed before we were allowed to begin eating, we would all

44

sit down to eat our meal: I have to say here, that the availability of food at Nazareth house was never an issue that I was ever aware of and I could never complain of any shortcomings in that department: The children were always very well fed.

There was one practice that was always allowed, whereby a child whose birthday fell on a particular day was permitted to take their plate down to the kitchen to have a special meal prepared; usually a fry up of some kind but always including, among other rare treats, a fried egg; a delicacy that we were not able to enjoy in the normal course of events: It was a delicacy that was only ever served to the children on special feast days: There was one period during my time at Nazareth house when I spent time tending to the hens in what was known as the 'chicken run': They had comfortably more than 100 birds there, so that the continuing lack of availability of eggs always remained a subject upon which I still continue to dwell, even up to this particular moment in time. I also spent as much time as I was allowed to do, helping the staff that worked in the kitchen; thankfully, I was always made welcome and tolerated there: It was a pleasant diversion from the normal routine that was convent life: I made many friends in there and spent many hours chatting or simply finding little jobs to do, and my friends in the kitchen were always willing providers on that score: Some sympathy maybe from the staff and the sister who always worked there, towards one mildly recalcitrant child who just wanted to keep his head down for a little while and was grateful for the opportunity, offered by 'jobs' in the kitchen, that enabled him to do so.

Personal abuse continued of course, and remained a normal part of daily life: It still remained integral with the house's normal life culture, continuing to persist as part of the normal operating function in the house, appearing to us to be as natural as any other acceptable group function, so that we all pretty much took it for granted as being the only way that the natural course of events within the house's social structure continued to proceed: Expressions of violence were usually most prevalent during times when we were all congregated together: The mere fact of us all being together in one place seemed most likely to engage those negative influences so that various people reacted in an inordinate manner; or perhaps it was due simply to the odd hectic rash that generally constituted boredom and a need for diversions of one kind or another, or perhaps it was just because of the pressing need to express an unrequited and inexplicable malice: One particular practice that I personally endured on more than one occasion involved the placing of a child's pudding directly on top of an unfinished dinner, and then compelling a child to eat both of the meals together: This was an event that happened, to my certain knowledge, on more than one occasion in the refectory: I was personally 'persuaded' to eat it all up in one go under threat of punishment, if I did not comply: At the very least I always tried to do my best, with the threat of violent retribution hanging over me: This activity meant that I would end up being violently sick; a reaction that only succeeded in encouraging the bullies even more: I don't recall it ever becoming a regular activity to be sure, but I do know that it happened personally, to me on more than one occasion; never mind the fact that many other children also endured the same kind of treatment as well. (Christmas pudding and dinner, eaten as one meal has never been the first choice in combinations, and the taste of it is one that I hesitate to recommend to anybody, not even to my worst enemy.)

Occasionally, treats arrived from the kitchen, crusty toast edges that had been sent over to the children, either from the nun's tables or as extras from the 'old' people; we never knew who it was, but we never really minded very much either: Anything that was a bit different was always a good enough treat at any time!

We were always alerted to any unpredictable situations, when the demeanour of one of the nuns might not have been the best kept secret at the time and it was probably prudent, in situations like that to steer a distant course, attempting, if at all possible, to keep the head down, metaphorically speaking, below the parapet, in case any kind of adverse reaction was seen to be forthcoming: The outcome of any of these onsets of adverse pique might not always have been as benign as that which might first have been hoped for: I can still recall one moment in particular, standing at the table in the refectory, waiting with all of the other children for 'grace" to begin, when I was observed by the nun in charge of the meal session at the time, tinkering with a salt cellar: Without even a word or any further hesitation, and in what seemed an unseemly outburst of unbridled petulance, she strode down to my table; grabbed the salt cellar and proceeded to pour a quantity of the stuff straight down my throat.

Duly chastened, I swallowed the salt and gave no more thought any more to it, proceeding with my meal as I normally did, after that event: It seemed, however that within the space of a few days the episode with the salt cellar had evolved itself into an essentially different situation altogether, with the consequence that my body's size began to increase to an abnormal degree. I cannot say that I was acutely aware of any of the changes to my body but I do remember that I was summarily sent to a bed in the infirmary to await a visit from the doctor: The other children actually took to calling me 'fatty' to which I took considerable exception, particularly since I, myself was unaware of any physical changes in my personal circumstances or appearance: What child ever bothers about mirrors anyway?

I used to think that it was somewhat ironic that if ever a doctor visited at the house, every aspect of the room would have been thoroughly cleaned and checked until it was deemed suitable to the purpose of the visit: I suppose it was one more practice that Irish people had brought back with them from the old country, since most of the nuns were of Irish descent anyway The whole situation of the illness had become one for which I was totally unprepared: I was after all unaware, in my own mind that I had even been ill at all: I was taken, eventually to the children's ward at Southend general hospital and placed there, in the care of some wonderful nurses.

The whole experience of hospitalisation was itself a rather strange affair for me: My first recollections of moving in to the hospital were of being placed into a bed, in a ward with several other children, and provided with various tasty foodstuffs; thinking to myself that maybe this hospital thing might not be so bad after all: Little did I realise the length of time that I would be incorporated into this strange new world. The time that I was kept in Southend general hospital actually extended to over a year and I was cared for by nurses that looked after me diligently, attending to my many and various needs: For all of the time that I was in the hospital I was confined to bed, which was ok by me: In all the time that I was in the hospital I was not allowed to leave my bed, and all of the care and the personal attention that I required was provided for me while I remained in what proved to be a bed borne position. I have to say that I probably enjoyed the time that I spent in a world that even time in heaven could not have competed with, and also a situation that I might not even have dared to dream of, in relation to another-wise recently past life: The nurses were kind and attentive and I was pampered and cared for constantly, with all of my needs and all of my wants provided for, waited on hand and foot and so fussed over: I loved it all! Why should I not have? This whole hospital experience was like the transition from the reality that had been life in a convent home, to a whole new caring culture that remained, if only as a temporary legacy; my own wonderful hospital bed: Indeed, it became the existence that improved life even beyond even my wildest dreams. Sadly, these same restrictions also insisted that I subsist on a salt-free diet for a whole year; an unpleasantly variable restriction that involved a dietary control that I never ever really grew that accustomed to: No more tasty meaty foods, that I had always so enjoyed: I was still allowed the questionable luxury of various different kinds of specialist foods and a preferential care regime that I became totally comfortable with, as well, at the end of the day.

Over and above all of these things however, it was possible to enjoy an alternative environment where people treated me with kindness and consideration. The staff were anxious always to please and provided me with their comfort, without any persuasion or any reason to threaten intimidation: For at least one significant year, I enjoyed all of the protection that I would ever require from a situation that had always been the fabric of my consciousness while I had lived within the confines of Nazareth house.

A sour note in this story has to be the mild resentment that I was forced to endure at my regular mealtimes as the smell of savoury salted meals wafted across the ward, towards my own bed, aggravating already tortured taste buds to distraction.

Eventually of course, I returned to Nazareth house again, after I eventually recovered sufficiently from my long illness: When I arrived back at the home, I occasionally received bundles of comic books from a kind person who had lived in Canada: One more quandary in the ongoing dilemma of who the mystery person might have been, who had taken the trouble to communicate with me at all, and about whom I had had no control and no knowledge, of what the name of that sender might have been, either.

There were significant consequences that still continued to relate to my stay in hospital, most of which I was not even aware of at the time: I still do not have a recollection, for instance of any of the events that occurred after my initial arrival at hospital, but I do recall that soon after my reception into hospital, my condition must have deteriorated to a point that I even received the last rites (to the uninitiated, the sacrament of 'Extreme Unction' and 'Confirmation') eventually to recover sufficiently, and to discover on waking up, that a priest was seated quietly beside my bed.

(There are seven Sacraments that exist in Catholic church dogma: Baptism, Confirmation, Holy Communion, Penance, Extreme Unction, Holy Orders and Matrimony: During our time on this Earth we are invited to avail ourselves of these Sacraments, so as to better engage with the benefits that Catholicism aims to provide: I can personally attest to the fact that I have been the recipient of all of these sacraments, except of course, the one of Holy Orders: Sadly, I never did quite achieve a priesthood, at the end of the day!)

The Sacrament of Extreme Unction involves the anointing of a body that is considered to be close to death, in the full and certain knowledge that as a consequence of this sacrament, the soul will never be committed to an eternal punishment in Hell: The blessing of 'Confirmation' was one more Sacrament that I was never able to qualify for in the convent due of my lack of a relevant knowledge of the catechism; so that the fact that I did actually receive it in the end, without even realising that it had been administered to me at the time, was just one more blessing that actually gave me pause to smile to myself, at the time that it happened.

The day finally arrived, close to the end of my stay in hospital, when I was finally allowed, after a year of restrictive care, to eat salted, and other regulated savoury foods again. I was still only permitted salt free kinds of bread that I had always been eating anyway, but the nurses were still very tolerant and kind to me. It must have been difficult for them to pander to all of my needs all of the time that I had been in their care and it was probably even more difficult for them to deal with a child who had himself became so adapted and so conditioned to hospital life with all of its intrinsic implications, as I had become: It is difficult to express my consummate joy at being able to eat those different types of food again, that I had for so long been denied either sight, taste or smell of, for over a year and for which I had continued to yearn, for so very long!

On the day that I was finally told that I could leave my bed, I was surprised to discover that I was unable to walk: Walking properly again now suddenly became the new priority in my life:

The importance of education while I was in hospital turned out actually, to be something of a non-event at the time: It was a situation, to be frank, about which I had never actually given too much thought: Sadly though, I never engaged in any normal educational activities during my stay in hospital, nor during that time was I ever offered any opportunities that might have enabled me to improve my education either, such as perhaps one-for-one tutoring, that might have helped me to some degree towards any future educational progress. I can't ever recall being contacted by any person, during my stay in hospital, from Nazareth house, that might perhaps have encouraged me towards a minimal degree of scholastic improvement: This lack of support included the lack of any educational stimulus from any other hospital sources either, that might have enabled me to at least pretend to maintain a workable level of other-school life. I do not recall reacting, one way or the other to the dearth of any procedures that might have been considered as formal education structure, of which I had already been regularly afflicted throughout most of my formative years while living at Nazareth house: During the year that I spent in hospital, the implications of all of that disparity were clearly reflected in any hopes that I might have nurtured, of any future educational progress.

I returned, finally to the regular fold of normal convent routine again: Therapeutic activities did proceed occasionally during the time that I was in hospital, that usually included some elementary craft work and other light creative diversions, aimed probably at relieving the prevailing boredom; always endemic in any hospital environment.

It is only fair to include the rider that any appreciation of a lack of educational sufficiency will only come home to its roost at a much later stage in a developmental career: Deficiencies become so much more highlighted with the continuing passage of time and the growing need for skills that might have been necessary in the future; a possible attainment of any future goals.

I have to add, in passing, that the period of time that I spent at Southend hospital, children's ward was at the very least, a year of wonderful seclusion from a lifetime that was entirely bereft of any aspect of an adverse environment that had been convent life: Gone were the threats of intimidation and the fear: I grew to appreciate that there were indeed systems and cultures in which people might actually express kindness and smiles, and the threat of intimidation took no part in what became ultimately my alternative utopia.

When I was finally discharged from Southend hospital I was then transferred to a convalescent home in Bexhill: An ok kind of place that catered for children of about my age that had also been seriously ill at some time in their own childhoods. It always surprised me that the nurses always seemed to be aware; even before I rose in the morning, whether I was anyway unwell or not and I would immediately be instructed on whether or not to remain in my bed. The issue of constant care was a factor in my life that I was not able, ever, to fully come to terms with or even to really get used to, as I actually felt quite well for most of the time, during my stay at this home but while I stayed there, they did actually take the best of care of me.

We occasionally took long walks down to the seaside at Bexhill: On one of my visits to the beach I walked far away from the beach, on to the extensive mud flats, while the tide was low, at that time. A Gloster Meteor aircraft was flying very low towards me, directly above my head and at a very high speed: Imagine my delight as I watched it approaching me: All I could see was a large silver shape that was its shiny metal body with silver engines and silver wings, and the loud roar when it passed directly over my head: I did not realise it at the time but the RAF had been engaging with high speed trials on that stretch of the coastline, at that time, in their pursuit of a world air speed record: The Royal Air Force HIGH SPEED FLIGHT had been active along this stretch of the coast for some time now and I still clearly remember watching this aircraft as it flew low, directly above my head.

After my convalescence at Bexhill, I returned eventually to Nazareth house and continued living with the other children again, much as though life in that establishment had never been any different for me: Readjustments within the home had however already begun to be introduced, regarding re-acclimatisation into a way of life that I had, for a while been enabled to escape from, for a while, but had now returned to, for it to engage with me once again: Who can say, as this period in the functioning of the house was also engaged with the process of change regarding new and revised arrangements, all relating, at the end of the day, to the ultimate well-being of the children:

Essentially, the changes involved reducing the size of one large group of children, that had always existed as a single entity, into what eventually became a subdivision into three smaller groups: The same arrangement applied as well to the dormitory sizes as well, when one large room that had provided beds for all of the children, was divided instead into three smaller ones.

I remember being rather excited about these new developments at the time and the children were all inclined to view these new arrangements in a generally positive light, perhaps because of the improved degree of personalisation that this new arrangement entailed, meaning that we might even be able to engage with each other on a more personal, and perhaps more amenable level, and perhaps even engage together on a more social level as well, with those nuns, but I am still not able recall whether that was ever really the case, or whether it ever it actually came to be so, at the end of the day.

As I have already told you, the provision of regular food at mealtimes, was never an issue at Nazareth house. The meals were always substantial and sufficient: I cannot ever remember nursing pangs of hunger: I have to add in consideration of that fact that I have grown to be an undemanding eater, having learned from an early age, always to make sure to eat whatever it is that is put in front of me, without the added temerity of complaint, is a prerequisite with which I have learned to live, throughout most of my young life.

Christmas was the most miraculous of times for the children: We were even provided with a fairy tale feast of a meal on Christmas day: We were all rewarded, when we walked into the refectory, with a vision of tables loaded to the gunwales with the most marvellous of food that could be imagined; spread out on the tables like a scene from some popular DISNEY fairyland scenario; it included blocks of ice cream, jelly, cakes and Lord knows what other delights, littering the tables to overflowing: It was, incredibly, the most wonderful vision to behold and it appeared to us like a glorious vision of magic, wonder and colour. Of course, this did all happen a long time ago, to be sure, but the memories of that moment are as vivid today as they were at that moment in time. While I am on the subject of Christmas, it was also the most wonderful of times for all of the children: Not a day would go by without regular outings being organised by local groups and organisations in the town: The children were taken to see pantomimes as well as to specially organised Christmas parties, arranged by people who were both kind and generous, intent only on making the day out that they had prepared for the children to be the most wonderful and memorable of occasions: There were so many of these events and it seemed like they went on forever, day after day, as if it was ever likely that there was a moment when we would ever grow tired of them. My deepest thanks go out to all of those kind people in Southend and I am sure that none of those children will ever be likely to forget any of their kindnesses either.

The American air force visited us every year as well, from their base at RAF Wethersfield, and that was always a special occasion for us. They brought with them items of clothing, fruit and of course a toy, for every child: It was always a special day for us and there was even one year when we all travelled together to their home base at Wethersfield instead. The children were all entertained together, inside a large aircraft hangar: I imagine that there must have been some 900 children from different homes, entertained in that hangar that day: While I was sitting, waiting with our own group, I expressed a personal interest, which was obviously alive and well, even at this young age, persuading one of the airman to allow me to go with him and see the aircraft: Together, we drove off, just the two of us; and I did actually see some F86 Sabres parked nearby, albeit just passing visits: I returned eventually to the hangar, on board a huge American fire engine that also brought Santa Claus, along with all of his presents, loaded up on the same truck: I really did feel a bit like a king, that day!

One particular treat that the Americans brought with them for us to eat, was an edible foodstuff called American pop corn: It was a salted variation on our own sweetened kind: None of the children actually liked it very much so that it was all left lying around, discarded and uneaten for the rest of the day: The irony of this tale, however, is that all of the children had come to the same conclusion, by the next day, that the popcorn was not really that bad after all; the consequence of that discovery being that none of us could get enough of the stuff, by the time the next day had arrived.

One fact that remained a constant in the home was the degree of camaraderie that maintained between the children: it wasn't so much admitted to, as subliminally understood: We didn't fight with each other and there existed a mutual accord that we all shared together and fully understood: Perhaps because we were aware that we were somehow different, in a similar way, without ever really understanding why; it remained just a natural fact of life: We shared, after all, much the same kind of environment and living condition, similar and yet so much together: It would always be the same with the children, and there perhaps lies a subliminal perception, that while we are different from everyone else, we were always the same to one another.

There was a song that we all knew and sang:- Please excuse the pronunciation:

"We are the 'Sahfend' boy's, We are the 'Sahfend' boy's"

"We use our manners, We spend our tanners"

"We are respected wherever we go."

"We go marching down the old back street."

"All the windows wide open:"

"All the lasses looking out"

"Get a brick and knock 'em' out!"

"We are the 'Sahfend' boys!"

'The old back street' being of course, "North road", that bordered the convent on one side.

CHAPTER 6

On bedtimes

B edtime was a regularly observed discipline and the children were always in their beds by six o clock each evening: The dormitory was a large sleeping space, filled with some thirty beds, the rest of the beds were distributed in smaller adjoining rooms: Every child was provided with a small bedside cabinet, placed beside his bed, but these items only arrived as later additions in the house, so that any personal belongings might be stored in them from time to time; a small concession I suppose, to a need for some semblance of personal privacy in the retention of personal keepsakes; possessions and personal identity, maybe: A popular practice that most of the children subscribed to, involved the decorating of the tops of their side tables with small doylies, ornaments and trinkets, so that they might perhaps be brightened up a little and perhaps encourage the pursuit of some semblance of personal individuality: The older boys still continued to rule the roost at night and one of the tasks, included as their responsibility was the one of getting the younger children into their beds and off to sleep: Unfortunately, the older boys had a little game of their own that they all enjoyed playing, that involved the swinging of a broom above the heads of the children, waving it at some considerable speed from side to side, above a particular child's head, at the same time as calling out his name: Eventually of course the child will respond by raising his head: The child that had been addressed always looking up to see who it is that has been calling to him, singularly unprepared for the shock that is awaiting him: What jolly fun they had, those boys, but this kind of activity existed as a par for the course at Nazareth house, insofar as the control of the children was concerned.

I still have many recollections of a recurring nightmare during my time at Nazareth house: The first indication of this, that I can recall, happened on one particular night when I was woken suddenly by a dreadful bellowing sound; an angry noise that assailed all of my senses and invading the space around my bed: I was so frightened by what seemed to me to be a dangerous and threatening presence that was confronting me with dangerous and aggressive intent and I knew that if I remained in my bed, it was going definitely going to attack me: The sound was so deafening to me and so malignant that it frightened me terribly: It was so tangible that all that I could think of to do was to run from my bed, and escape from the dormitory as quickly as I could, and from this encroaching menace: I ran away, blindly, down the long, stone tiled passage towards the toilet block, where I could hide and possibly avoid this threat, seating myself inside one of the cubicles: I might then finally avoid whatever it was that had pursued me: I was gratefully relieved and surprised then, when I realised that it had not continued to pursue me into the cubicle but seemed content instead to linger on the outskirts of the long passage: I waited there in breathless silence for what seemed to me to be an indeterminate amount of time: I cannot state with any certainty how long it was that I remained concealed inside the toilet but I can state with certainty that for me the process of hiding myself in there extended into a long and failing memory. This nightmare episode repeated itself on several other occasions after that first night, always beginning with the same visit and always continuing with the same levels of spite and aggression, continuing constantly to intimidate me as I continued to hide myself away from the, menace in an abject terror: Many were the nights that I spent, that seemed always to drag on and seemed always to happen at about the same time as well, in that dark and cold toilet cubicle, listening to that infernal noise with the same terrified dread, waiting only to be assailed in the confined space that extended just beyond my safe field of vision: I knew only that it was still out there, waiting its opportunity to inflict whatever it wanted to do to me: I knew only that it was simply content to watch and to wait: I cannot admit to ever having seen it, face to face but neither did I ever dare to confront it on any sort of personal level either: I just remained content to stay hidden from it, night after night: It actually became easier with time for me to conceal myself, and to keep on hoping that it might not come any closer to me than it already appeared to be doing: After what seemed an interminable amount of time, sitting and waiting in the cubicle, certainty would finally prevail sufficiently that I would brave a tentative glance, peering out and waiting, for what seemed like an eternity, until I was finally satisfied enough that it had gone away again, leaving me alone: After a while, I would finally pluck up sufficient courage, deciding that it might actually be safe enough for me to emerge now, and return once more to my bed: The nights were many, after that initial event, that were spent cowering in that cold toilet, waiting with a fearful dread, until I was finally able to decide whether it was safe enough for me to creep back to my own bed, again.

As often as this issue progressed, I still continued being harassed by this 'entity', but the final outcome always seemed to be the same: I came finally, to the conclusion that this demon had to be confronted, one way or the other: I was aware that whatever this thing was, or even what it intended finally to do to me, it had never actually caused me any harm in any of these episodes: I concluded therefore, that it was perhaps time for me to face this threat to my personal wellbeing, head on, if only for the purpose of settling the matter, once and for all: On this particular night therefore, as I sat, waiting in my cubicle, having fled from my bed again, with my customary fright, listening to this thing again, all of the while; the noise and the bellowing still continued, as it always did, to torment me: I opted, therefore, in that moment, to step out of the cubicle to confront this menace, face to face: It was in that moment that I realised that there was actually nothing there at all for me to see or to perceive of and I could no longer see or hear that awful presence near me anymore: Thankfully for me, after that awful final confrontation with the 'demon' it never did come back to torment me again; and after that last night I was never ever disturbed by it, ever again.

I have already discussed at some length the normal preparations that we were all involved with before getting into our beds, reciting prayers, the last thing that we did in the evening and the first thing that we did every morning.

One issue that continued to have more than the usual impact on my life, occurred when I was about nine or ten years old: It involved the continual curse of bed wetting: Bed wetting was a common enough occurrence within the confines of the house: That is not to say that it was not frowned upon and derided by the powers that be: The degree of punishment and retribution that were regularly distributed to any unfortunate children that had been unable to control their bladders, was singularly commensurate with whoever was in the position of authority at that moment, to distribute the most effective of admonishments to any unfortunate sinner that had had the temerity to soil their bed in the first place: The punishment normally took the form of either outright derision in front of the rest of the children, or having one kind of violent punishment or another, inflicted upon them, again in front of everybody else, the intention being to inflict the maximum effect in terms of severe humiliation. As far as I was concerned, bed wetting always happened during the night, of course, when I was asleep and I would be woken finally by that same damning sensation that I had for a long time, come to recognise, from many earlier repetitions of the same event: It always began with what seemed to me to be like the re-living an old dream, and it always ended with the same unpleasant sensation as its finish: It was not actually total dream experience, per se but was instead the repetition of an old familiar nocturnal discovery Yet again; the dream that I wake from is not actually a bad dream at all but is instead the familiar sensation that signals release, telling me that I had, in all likelihood, probably wet the bed, yet again, while waking me up at the same time.

A hurried glance under the bed, and on to the floor usually confirmed my worst fears: Armed with the benefit of previous experience, I leap quickly from my bed to deal with the issue: The prevention of discovery and the avoidance of any complications that might have ensued as a result of this, would remain as the driving force for the prevention of any repercussions that might then have arisen, had this particular 'misdemeanour' actually been discovered by any of the nuns or the senior boys. The first order of business then, called for the removal of any discriminating trace of evidence that still remained on the floor: After that had been cleared up, I then turned my attention to the wet mattress, turning it over quickly, to conceal any wet stains that might still have been exposed: It is worth mentioning that this usually happened at about the same time every night, so that I was pretty well assured of the privacy that I required, providing that I kept all of this activity to as low a level of noise as was reasonably possible: Total secrecy was always the most essential of prerequisites in this particular exercise since the nuns would be asleep in what were described as their 'cells'; private enclosures, positioned for them to sleep in, in each of the dormitories: After the initial 'removal' exercise had been completed I quickly took the soiled bottom sheet off the bed and carried it along the stoned tiled toilet passage that I have already referred to earlier, towards a large airing cupboard, located in the same general area of the toilet block, inside of which a hot water boiler was also located.

It was a rather large water tank, and the water that it contained was usually kept at quite high heat levels, for certain reasons, but it still served as the factor best suited to my particular purpose: The tank was quite large in size, and I was sufficiently small, that I was able to squeeze myself between it and the enclosing wall: Positioned between the tank and the wall, it then became a simple matter for me to bide my time and wait, within the boiler cupboard, for the pyjamas that I was wearing, to dry; There was almost sufficient access in the back of the cupboard that contained this tank, that I was able to slide myself right in at the back of the tank and the wall and still lodge myself against its metal body: It was rather uncomfortable at times because there were always variations in the heat of the water in the tank, but necessity will always be the servant of survival and that most essential of requirements it will always usually enable success to prevail in the end.

When that particular exercise was finally over and my pyjamas had dried on me sufficiently, all was ready again for me to then drape the soiled sheet over the top of the tank until it was finally dry as well: When this task was completed all that remained for me to do was to creep back to my bed again with nobody any the wiser: I would never have suggested that it was the most practical of exercises to execute, at any time; the water tank sometimes got quite hot, particularly if it had not been much utilised recently: At times though, when the tank did actually get too hot, it still remained as the most practical of solutions of what would otherwise have been the most difficult of situations for me to deal with, had that fact ever been discovered: I would say that in general terms, my survival skills must have been moderately well tuned, perhaps by relative experience, as I was never once discovered in any of my nightly escapades, for however long a time it was that they actually took place.

Before the transformation of the buildings structure into the redesign philosophy that became the new children's areas and to which I have recently referred, there existed two large single dormitories that, between them accommodated all of the children in the house: That meant that there were probably thirty or so children in each dormitory: It was an arrangement that altered significantly when the new improvements had been introduced into the set-up, whereby the system that the convent actually functioned by, in relation to the care of the children, altered radically, forever.

Many of the improvements that took place at Nazareth house involved substantial changes to the basic set up of the children's areas and the reorganisation of all of the layouts, that I suspect, were encouraged by radical thinking coordinators who's only intention remained the general improvement in the living standards of the children in these homes. I do believe that there had always been proponents for these positive changes in the area of the houses in which children that were brought up, might have better engaged their minds and their well-being so that a better understanding of a healthy outlook on their lives might have been more congenial to their happier and more successful existence in their futures.

The most obvious indications that these changes were actually taking place were the alterations from one single large group of children into several smaller ones of three 'groups' which then continued operating, still as a single, integrated unit within the larger groups: on the whole, a vaguely convoluted system that, nevertheless seemed to work quite well: I wonder how much of an impetus to those changes in the structure of life in the homes were instigated by events that were perhaps exacerbated by my own recent hospitalisation: one more subject that might have been worthy of mild conjecture, I suppose!

The large single dormitories with which we had all become accustomed were also improved with the addition of partitions, so that they were also recreated into three separate smaller 'dorms': The children were also divided into smaller groups so that from that moment on, the concept of one large group of children, all living together as a single entity, became the retiring symbol of a past history; lost finally in a time that will remain forever as forsaken legacy; hopefully in this case, more lost than forgotten. I was surprised at the speed with which these changes did come into effect: Some whispers had been circulating for some time about these stories, but as with most tales, the truth will only ever lie in their actual veracity. The children all viewed these possible new developments with a cautious circumspection, probably due to proposals such as this always somehow being relayed as questionable rumour, finally to be dismissed as unbelievable and uncertain maybe's, promising only as new prospects, by the children themselves.

The principles of these same improvements also applied to mealtime arrangements as well: The children, as a whole, took to these changes very positively, as the concept of smaller groups of children living together, instead of in one large one, meant that the degree of intimacy made mutual inter-relationships between them all, that much more viable and much more comfortable to deal with as well. I must say that when I recall the proposals that included the total redesign of the layout of the children's areas, I do not recall any reaction, either positive or negative except one of cautious anticipation, at these new proposals that were being projected.

With hindsight, it is reasonable to suppose; in any event, that any kind of reaction that remained in the positive, that was being introduced in the house, would probably have diminished with time by the years of emotional repression and the abiding culture of religious obeisance that had never really attempted to cultivate the exercise of original thought and expression, endemic within the original climate of the home.

These new changes all came about during the years including 1958 to 1961 and were on the whole fairly substantial alterations: To begin with, the children were all transferred to different schools that were not actually located within the confines of the convent: As I have already told you, this new education process began for me when I was sent further up the road to a school called St. Helens RC School, reasonably close to the convent.

My educational processes continued into my later years and included the time that I later spent at St. Thomas More high school, which singular event I have already also touched upon.

The significance of all of these new changes rested in the culture that it engendered for all of the children who had stayed at Nazareth house: I cannot say that I ever perceived of the changes to this living condition as being real improvements 'per se' as much as I perhaps should have, due to the processes that had affected the way this new evolving structure was altering both my outlook and my emerging perspectives: Most of the changes to my life at that time, if that had been in any way possible, would have been seen simply as an unwillingness to accept the consequences of these new conditions that I had been accustomed to living with, for such a long time and also because of the way that those changes might ultimately have affected me anyway, in the long run.

I think now, with the benefit of hindsight, that these proposed changes to a system that had probably not been the best and most efficient one available at the time and involved the bringing up of large groups of children, incorporating, for its purpose, many of the restrictive and repressive practices; engendering in the end, a new and more effective culture of care in the home and leading to a more suitable coexistence for all of the children, in the execution of their daily lives and in all of their futures.

Consequences

T he mental adjustments involved in having to adapt to a regulated existence within any institution will probably take a great deal of time for the inmates of that institution to become accustomed to: Children, by their very nature and because of their young age, adapt eventually and have a natural resilience to any way of life that has been offered to them; a consideration that is hopefully expedient to their emotional needs and to their ultimate survival as well: The inevitability of repetition and the exposure to any of the rigours of regulation, at such a young age only make the whole exercise that much more amenable to them, in the end.

It had become an imposition of circumstances, always accepted without question, as it was indeed required to be, and the requirement that is imposed with it, simply becomes one more part of a repressive whole; that living thing within an institution that makes life such an available circumstance and such a normal way of life to live with, at the end of the day.

The imposition of religious tenets and the application of its governance through the use of them, in all of our daily lives, only serves to confirm those devious mental impositions: Constant declarations concerning hell and damnation, only serving to cement a fear that had already been installed from the earliest age, ensuring that we all continued to believe that all kinds of punishment will be visited upon 'naughty' children by God: So it was that children were raised always to remain compliant, fear of fear being the ultimate tool with which obedience without effort can always be achieved.

The basic procedure, of having new shoes fitted, on odd occasions, was a typical case in point, where the issue of consensual compliance was concerned: Normally, new shoes were provided after a reasonable period of time, but the practice of measuring them up and fitting them on to a child's foot, properly and safely, fell by the wayside as the object of a work in progress: The fitting of feet into shoes might sound, on the face of it, to be a simple enough exercise to perform, just so long as reasonable care is taken to ensure that the fit of the shoe is an acceptable one in terms of both its width and its length: What actually happened in fact, was that a cursory press of the thumb onto the toe was felt, seeking for an acceptable indentation, and that is what would have been deemed sufficient indication that the shoe was indeed of an acceptable size and fit, insofar as the nun in question was concerned. The child would then be sent on his way with a dismissive wave and a new pair of shoes to call his own, with never any consideration of complaint or with any question or doubt that the shoes might have been in any way uncomfortable or otherwise unsuitable for the feet: Any temerity that might have been indicated; perhaps by actually expressing an opinion on the subject, would simply not have been tolerated: Tacit subservience had always remained as the abiding benchmark of due humility and we had always to be humble and compliant in any way that it suited them for us to be: Sadly, the reality of this particular turn of events often involved altogether different conclusions: In the fullness of time, long after I had finally left the confines of the convent, problems with my feet began to develop: As time moved on, it became clearer to me that the fitting of wrong size shoes for far too long a time, during my childhood, meant that my feet had subsequently become irreparably damaged; the toes had become compressed together, ultimately creating the issue of distorted toes: The resultant pain that any direct contact involved me in, was simply more than I could bear. The only option eventually left to me that might have enabled me to alleviate this discomfort, involved having a small toe surgically removed: For me the amputation finally ended what had become a somewhat difficult episode with a fair degree of suffering that I could not allow to continue any longer: Thus was unfortunately the way of things and I can only smile now at the sad inevitability of it all.

With hindsight, I have to wonder how much of an issue the question of properly fitted shoes was, in relation to identical issues that must have prevailed among all of the other children that had also been issued with new shoes as well, also at various times in their pasts, in all of those same homes.

There was a perceptible increase in the levels of anticipation in the home, as summer time approached: During this time, we were able to look forward to two-week long summer breaks, away from our own home: All we knew for certain was that we would be staying in a different children's home and the children from that home would be coming to stay in ours: The anticipation involved in just visiting a different place and staying in a different house with different people, was an exciting prospect for all of us.

Departure day finally arrived and the excitement was almost palpable as two large coaches turned up the drive; the children all piling on board to secure their seats: I was content just to take a moment or two to marvel at the cavernous size of the boots on those coaches, with all of the stuff that was waiting to be loaded, piled up outside. A personal characteristic that has not always endeared me to my contemporaries is that more than once I have succeeded in irritating both my enemies and my friends by asking questions that they may not ever have been entirely comfortable with the idea of having to think seriously about: Any opportunities for interactions with children from the new home were somewhat restricted, but we could still wave at them occasionally, even at what were considered safe distances: In actual fact, fraternisation was never actually encouraged very much anyway, particularly if it happened that females were coming to stay at the house.

An event was held at the house every year called 'pound and gift day': It involved the public being invited to visit the home, and to be escorted around the house by the children. For the boys, it meant meeting with as many of the visitors as possible, as rapidly as was possible; introducing ourselves and accompanying them around the house, while displaying every possible courtesy to the visitor at the same time: In return, the children were rewarded with small financial considerations: A few of the boys actually did quite well out of it: I recall being taken aback somewhat when one of the nuns told me to purloin certain items that they had eyed, among the contributions that had been donated by the visitors (the reason that it was called 'pound' or 'gift' day: Often visitors brought gifts, including items of food.) some of which the nuns had already secured for themselves: They would then quickly hide them away: I regret to admit that it rather pleased me to do these things, for the sake of sad acquiescence, meaning that I might yet walk away feeling a little bit better in myself, even if it was only for a while!

We spent a lot of our time playing in the large field that was at the rear of the house: It incorporated all of the normal facilities that children always enjoyed playing on; climbing frame, roundabout and of course swings; in fact, all of the trappings that might have been included in any normal children's playground: The field beyond the playground was for the most part left to its own devices as far as any ground maintenance was concerned so that the grass and the weeds grew pretty much as they pleased, largely uncontrolled: The field was generally filled with stinging nettle plants, mixed in with the normally long grass: We didn't play very often in that stuff! One odd trick, concerning the long grass that we did learn however, in the course of playing our war games in the field, was that great things could be achieved simply by tying the strands of long grass together so as to trip up the 'enemy' in our battles, when they were trying to 'fight' us: Quite effective it was too!

One boy, who was a particular friend of mine, lost his spectacles in the field towards the far end; the part of the field, particularly overgrown with nettles, and after some discussion, it was decided that they were probably lost somewhere in a part of the field that was seriously overgrown: After some thought about how they might be recovered, a solution was finally agreed, by the nuns: It was proposed that the children be persuaded to crawl along in a line through the long grass and the nettles (a la floor polishing!) in an organised search to recover them: There were some misgivings among the children about this particular proposal as we had little or no chance of avoiding any of the nettles if this little plan of theirs was put into effect: We all wore short trousers as a matter of course, during the day, so that the idea of crawling through a field full of nettles left us a little short on enthusiasm: Needless to say, we did eventually proceed with the idea, in any event and also needless to say, we all did suffer considerably as a result of the experience: Eventually, we found the glasses, I suppose but I do not recall how long a time that it took us: You can only imagine how pleased I was to see those spectacles again, though not, needless to say, so happy with the boy who had lost those spectacles, in the first place!

In about 1959, some female children arrived to stay at the house, in their own section of the convent: They were all deliberately quarantined, away from the boys. We were of course aware of their presence as they surely would have been of us as well: We were able to interact with them occasionally, but on a level of what was considered to be a safe and uncompromising distance: The whole conception of any girl being this close to a boy must have been one that was total anathema to the nuns and was probably tolerated at all, only with a considerable degree of social and reluctant duress: I would have liked to have been a fly on the wall at the meetings when it was finally agreed that girls might actually be accommodated in the same building as boys: I still recall the fascination with which we viewed this whole prospect; that real girls might actually be coming to live in the same house as the rest of us.

Unbelievable as it seems now, I actually got to kiss one of those girls: It was the first ever kiss of my life and it must have been in the cause of that one moment that insanity took control of what would normally have been the caution of reason: I still shudder to think what might have happened to me, had I ever been discovered: I still recall the moment when I approached her and asked her to join me behind a far wall, (how crass is that?) near to the outside of the building: I don't understand now, how it was that she agreed to meet me at all, in the first place; a fact that even today I still don't fully understand: It turned out to be the most wonderful of moments that I can ever recall: It had become almost a kind of madness, but wonders of wonders, she even agreed to meet me at another time! I obviously remember that first kiss, so much, with a longing and a desperation: I can still remember the danger of the moment as well though, and the risk that I took at that time, hoping against hope that if I was very lucky, I might even get away with the whole thing, in the end: To the casual reader it will probably appear to be just another reckless desire for a first kiss, but I can still recall every moment of that encounter, and I will probably continue to do so to the end of my days: I still ask myself how it was that I found the courage, in those dangerous and restrictive times, to even dare consider a proposition such as this one, at all. Wonder of wonders, I actually got around to kissing her sister as well: Don't ask me how it was that I was able to proposition two young girls behind the privacy of a convent wall: It is not as though it was something that I would normally have opted to engage in: I must explain that this was the pursuit of a kiss and the reckless danger that it involved: We both engaged with this mischievous exercise, probably with the full knowledge that this, as a dalliance would not be allowed to proceed beyond the grounds of what we had both considered to be a polite social interaction; at least that was how I had felt that it might have been at the time, anyway. I would have been more disposed to behaving in a controlled and deliberate manner, particularly where engagements with dangerous opposites were concerned. I can only assume that the combination of females and opportunity plus the pressure of interactive hormones, at the time, must have been sufficient reason to activate this temporary lunacy, stimulating it effectively to utter distraction. The girls were always carefully chaperoned by the nuns so that all I was ever able to do was to content myself with accepting that rare opportunities might still have presented themselves if I was sufficiently prepared to wait long enough for an opportunity such as this to come my way: Moments will always occur, in this construct that is life if you are heady enough that you are able to grab them when the moment is right: That same young lady agreed to meet with me again at a different time, but sadly that glorious dalliance remained as our final real moment, and was the day when my great adventure had finally run its course.

As I reflect on this period of my life at Nazareth house, I appreciate now, how dangerously we sometimes must have lived and the risks that we must sometimes have taken: How insane the whole concept of risk avoidance must have seemed at that time, and yet, with the benefit of hindsight, how wonderful those deviations from rigid stipulation cultures actually were; memories that I continue to cherish for the rest of my life: It was a time for experiences and most astonishingly of all, they often involved actions that were never ever discovered, an alarmingly rare distinction that still amazes me to this day; because if there was one fact that was ever certain at Nazareth house it was that misdemeanours were promptly discovered by those observer souls at their vantage points throughout the house, and would just as promptly have been reported on: I still wonder whether, after all of these years, either of those girls still can remember the excitement of that particular chase as well as I still can or even with as much of a permanently mental smile.

Pocket money was an irregular but intermittent distraction for us, usually distributed at some point in the day, on a Saturday afternoon. Too often it was pocket money that never even materialised, and lingering in the vicinity of a nun; expecting to be distributing the money, would not have made one ha'porth of difference, whether it ultimately came our way, or not, in the end!

When we did actually receive any pocket money, it was normally allotted at 'thruppence' for the junior boys and 'sixpence' for the senior boys.

(That equates to one and a quarter-pence and two and a half pence at that time.) then it was off to the corner shop to spend it as quickly as possible before it could be otherwise purloined.

I must have been about twelve years old when a number of the boys were selected to go to live in Australia: A few of the boys were chosen to take the long journey by ship and I remember noting then that, apart from the new clothes and the new suitcases with which they had all been provided, they were going away on what appeared to me to be the most exciting of journeys, to a new country and a new and exciting future: They would also be getting away for ever more, from this place: It seemed to our eyes to be not entirely a bad thing at all, for them: It seemed to us that they were being presented with a wonderful new opportunity: You lucky boys! I can still recall the envy that I felt for those boys at the time! Hindsight suggests, however, that since those early days, full of glowing optimism and opportunity, my longings for any future good fortune that they might themselves have been blessed with, have perhaps been misplaced with regard to what had been their possible future and any of the subsequent achievements that they might once had hoped to have attained, as a result.

Sundays were often spent going for long walks in the afternoon: We often walked together, hand in hand through the town. I don't ever recall being comfortable with this exercise as we all trooped along the pavement, usually towards the seafront area and the space known as the 'cliffs', a hilly grassy area that extended the length of the seafront and covered large tracts of the land above it. We actually used to enjoy visiting the 'cliffs' where, for a while, we were able to escape from the direct observations of the nuns, with our own reasonable degrees of privacy, at least for a while; but I did on the whole resent the impression that I was always made aware of, that we all seemed to represent, in terms of our novelty value, the fact that we were something of a curiosity for many of the staring townspeople.

There was a railway bridge on the way home, over which we passed on our way home and we often stopped to watch the steam trains as they pulled out of Southend central station, in the distance: We enjoyed watching and waiting as the trains puffed towards us, passing beneath the bridge that we were standing on: We liked to rush blindly across the road to the other side, so as to catch it again as it exited the other side, with its gush of black smoke: It never occurred to any of us, in those days that we might ever have been in danger from approaching cars: It was a situation at the time, where there was never a need to give it that kind of consideration.

These walks usually took about two hours and I suppose the only advantage that might have been gleaned from them was that they at least provided light relief from the daily tedium that was the normal agenda on a Sunday.

The activities for a normal Sunday began, usually after breakfast, began with cleaning and scrubbing floors in the toilet cubicles and the passage ways: These were all hard stone floors that unfortunately were always more inclined to be dirty and more unpleasantly soiled, particularly with the unmentionable materials that found their way into the secret crevices that make every toilet cubicle the unpleasant harbinger of everything that is remotely distasteful, which they usually do: Using large bars of carbolic soap and scrubbing brushes, one can liberally scrub a floor and clean around the bowl until it is deemed satisfactory: We became singularly adept at this task, often having to repeat the exercise as well, for reasons that we usually did not always fully understand; but ultimately, they remained the kind of tasks that we most tried to avoid doing, all together, if we could.

Polishing wooden floors were an altogether different and more time consuming activity: One of the boys would begin the task by spreading wax over the whole area of the floor, after which we would all kneel down on the floor with our heads touching the wall and our cloths ready in hand, to move together in a coordinated fashion: "All together, swing together, left, right, left, right." and so would we proceed, working backwards on our knees until we had reached the other end of the room when we would turn around and repeat the whole exercise, over again, and again, and again; ad infinitum, in fact, until the nun in charge had expressed herself satisfied with the finish of the floor: I should add that this really was a rather efficient process at the end of the day, when it came to getting floors beautifully waxed and polished: Labour intensive, to be sure, but effective!

After the work was all done, the children would then begin choir practice, a prolonged affair that usually involved all of the children as well the senior boys: The children would all gather together around the piano, in the playroom where we would begin by practicing our scales and several other variations on the same theme, just to establish voice control: After all of that was done, we would sing a mass or practise a new hymn, or maybe just a piece of plain chant. This period of practice continued for some two hours, sufficient time for us to complete the remainder of the morning. After we had finished choir practice, we then engaged with darning and repairing socks or making any other repairs that required our attention; the maintenance of clothes, both for ourselves and for our charges: Each senior boy had a 'charge'; a junior child whose care we were responsible for, even to the extent of ensuring that they were properly cleaned and bathed, at appropriate times. When we were of an age to be responsible for these children; (usually about 11 years old) that child remained in our 'charge' for the rest of the time that we were together in the home. Every child was allotted a number of his own that he carried with him all of the time that he lived in the home. The advantage that existed with this particular system was that all of the children's clothing was readily identifiable due to the number on the clothing. The whole arrangement meant that each item was attributed to one particular child and there was never any difficulty in identifying an article of clothing and subsequently being aware of the child to whom it belonged. It was a system that ensured that any item of clothing could be tracked at any point in the distribution of that item. The responsibility for charges also extended to ensuring that they were properly washed and dressed every morning and every night, day, as well as ensuring that their clothes were always maintained in as reasonable an order as possible: A bit of a task on its own, sometimes!

Bath times were a different exercise altogether: The bathroom was a large spacious area with wash sinks placed all around the room: Two baths were positioned in the centre of the room, on one of the end walls: The bath was filled at the start of a bathing session: Two of the boys would then have the task of standing in attendance at the bath while the first boy climbed into the water at the end of the bath and stood ready, waiting for his legs to be washed: The first boy would wash his legs: He wore, for this purpose a small slip that covered all of his private parts: With the benefit of hindsight, it is hard to believe that the children were ever properly cleaned in the areas where it actually mattered, as a consequence of this particular practice. The first boy, at the back, would then take himself up to the front of the bath and sit down to have the top part of his body washed while another boy then climbed in behind him, waiting for his turn to be bathed: All the first boy needed to do finally was climb out of the bath to a waiting towel (yes! They had those, as well!) to be finally dressed in his pyjamas, ready to go to bed.

CHAPTER 8

Aftermath

Consequences are the inevitable plague of actions that might not have been considered important enough at the time that they were initially instigated: What an unwholesome travesty of errors and erstwhile disasters these questionable decisions leave in their wake, for their beneficiaries to rue over, in the years and even the decades that will continue to haunt them.

It would be hard for me to put a pin in a timeline, that might have indicated the beginnings of damage that might have hindered anything that might have been considered normal developmental processes, during the time that still remained of my life, and particularly from the time that I finally left the confines of Nazareth house, but it is easier to date those life moments from the time it was that I finally began to realise that those rules that I had believed I would be able to live by in the real world were not actually going to operate as well for me as I had hoped that they might, when my first real push at life in the raw, actually came to shove.

When I finally left Nazareth house it was with a keen anticipation and optimism that this garden of new life existence, now laying out before these star-struck eyes, would probably soon be filled with people who were kind and understanding, rather than with people with whom I had, for so long shared such a different kind of upbringing and such a different kind of coexistence, so recently.

The reality, of course, was that the rules that people live by in the real world are the ones that I remained singularly unfamiliar with and were actually quite a bit different from the ones that I had always been led to expect and recognise; but it was also those same rules that I had always done my best to live by, in my own past.

I concluded, with some reluctance that humans, by dint of my own evolved assumption of their own understanding of the natural order of things; the details of which I had myself not been privy to, were maintained as part of that same natural ability, a willingness that they need, to exploit any person that they perceive of as being weaker than themselves: I might well have been disappointed at the time when I realised that dealing with people, and expecting to be welcomed by them with arms as open as my own had been, was a delusional expectation that was probably never actually going to see the light of day, in this real life scenario.

My naivety and my willingness to grasp at the false offerings of every hand that was held out to me, with frozen smiles and broken promises, only meant that I was constantly having to deal with the repeated mockery of falsified rejections and undisguised derisions.

Occasionally a person would appear who showed me a genuine kindness, but heaven help me, I found myself questioning their motives in the end, more than I did the reality that had been their unqualified generosity at the time, so that I probably appeared somewhat detached in my own personal dealings with that person, at the end of the day as well: Trust in human nature was an instinct that never really bore any of its fruit for me, in the pursuit of purposeful relationships with my fellow human beings, and even more particularly, if they were some of the female kind as well.

It is worth adding in consideration of this assessment of my own shortcomings, that I found myself to be a demanding and selfish suitor in terms of my own perceived needs and wants and perhaps suffered, in the raw from selfish requirements that in no way related to the reality that still remained as abiding principle in this life; that all other human inconsistencies normally operate in exactly the same way as well.

The most disturbing realisation of all was a discovery that had more than a little impact on my life than any other factor of significance: Briefly put; it was a continually confusing relationship with the people of the fairer sex: I was always aware that this was a problem that had not been exclusive to my tenure at Nazareth house and has existed to some degree, for a long time since then, as well: It did however, became more apparent, after I finally left Nazareth house and it expressed itself, in its darkest form as a glaring insecurity about anything that might have involved relationships with females: It persisted as an inability to comfortably interact in any kind of interchange, exacerbated by an overwhelming fear of rejection: Perhaps it was just that I had spent too long acceding to a stilted form of regulation from people who controlled all the aspects of my existence and my mind, without requiring either question or thought that might have elicited corresponding responses, or that I have ever been comfortable in dealing with, on an amicable level: Perhaps I elected, subconsciously, to elevate all of these people to levels of esteem to which they were perhaps not entitled, and now, I have to admit, were probably not even qualified for: In simple terms, I have been deflected throughout my life, by personal afflictions with which I have been invested but which have only served to hinder me since that time, for most of my life: Significant personal issues have certainly stemmed from various events in my early life, possibly relating to more direct concerns that, unfortunately, I have been forced to live with, at a physical level: For my extended lifetime, I am still burdened with a persistent hand tremor that has probably affected my confidence levels, for as long as I can remember and while most people are sufficiently well adjusted as not to comment on this particular condition, the continuing persistence of these tremors remain as inescapable legacies of the consequence of past events that I must still continue to persevere with, without ever understanding the cause for what still remains, today, as irritating emotional cast offs. I would certainly be more comfortable in my understanding of this condition if I was able to discover what those circumstances might have been, in some vague past historical mantra, that might have caused this situation to develop and persevere as it has done for such a long time in the first place: But then again, would I really be better off if I was actually to be in possession of that knowledge, at the end of the day?

The undesirable effects of life experience, including hospitalisation, when I was younger, were probably contributory factors in other health conditions that still reflect on my personal well-being to this day: I am assured, by doctors, that my kidneys will never be as healthy as they might once have been, but I do sometimes feel that perhaps this is just one more aspect of life that I must continue to live with as the result of vagrant circumstances relating to events that occurred in my past: Memories of hospital life have to include the misery, every day of people arriving at my bed with nasty implements of various sizes and lengths, usually to extract blood but also for various other daily liberties that they were allowed to take with my body: The sight of a needle, even to this day, still fills me with dread and alarm: While I am obviously required to tolerate the application of these objects on the odd occasion that injections are called for, I still have to look away whenever they are being applied.

So is it that you dear reader, might yet divine that any preparation that we all were led to believe, was considered adequate to the suitability of me coping with a life that might have been substantially different, in the real world, from what was, in fact, a far cry from the reality that is the truth that I was actually presented with, when the facts that I was seeking, were finally understood: The reality, of course is that my final discharge from Nazareth house meant a comfortable dispensation of all further responsibility by the nuns for any future care of me, and of any further concerns about my future well-being as well: At the risk of harping on about the predicament that I now find myself in, in this life, riddled with all of the emotional accoutrements that had served me so well while I was living within the confines of that institution; they have no place whatever in the real world that now exists beyond these four walls.

So does this little tale finally come to its close, but not without one final footnote concerning some inter-related later dealings that involved my real family.

In about 1980 I contacted the 'Salvation army'; a charitable organisation, with a view to contacting my mother: I requested their services in the hope that I might discover if I could develop any personal contact conditions regarding me getting in touch with her: I later received a reply from them informing me that she did not wish to see me but that 'mother and daughter' were well. Imagine my delight at discovering that I actually had a real sister in this world: I decided however, at that point, not to pursue my search any further, but to leave the matter where it lay, at that point.

It was a full ten years before I took any further action, when, in the course of a conversation with a private investigator I became involved enough to explain the non-going situation with my parents, to him. He agreed, for a price, to recover whatever information he could about my family: While his work was satisfactory up to a point, in terms of the research that he claimed to have undertaken, he did involve me in some peripheral difficulties, caused by some of his questionable operational procedures: He certainly made contact with my family but he continued, for the period of his communication with them, to pretend that he was actually me: There were, as a consequence some complications that arose when I actually got to meeting with them face to face: We actually met for the first time at the Tower Hotel in London and I found myself defending the cavalier approach that was employed by the investigator: I did find my sister to be a delightful and charming person, as was her husband and I was overjoyed at actually meeting them: My pleasure must have been truly palpable and she was everything I could ever have dreamed that she might have been: I truly felt that this new life was going to lead me into a new kind of personal renaissance, leading me eventually into a whole new world of social relationships: I was so overjoyed at the prospect of these new events that were expanding my horizons, even before these star filled eyes had even been fully opened.

We met again as a family at their home and we both exchanged photographs: Everything was cordial but the whole relationship remained naturally rather distant, but then, that was probably to be expected: My optimism however was still sky high and I looked forward to a future that promised me a new and mutual cordiality, whatever that would eventually bring to us; I even discovered during our meeting that I also had a brother as well: This was just getting better and better by the minute!

Soon after the meeting, my sister and her husband both went off on a world cruise while their move to a new house in Ascot, was completed: She wrote occasionally to me during this time and I always awaited her letters with an anxious anticipation.

We were invited to visit at the house soon afterwards with all of my family but, to my deep shame and regret I never did take my family there that day: I regret to say that I was just not ready for that visit and I behaved shamefully as a result, not even contacting her to apologise that I was not going to be there: I phoned the next day with the intention of apologising and was shocked at being greeted with a verbal lashing that stunned and upset me severely, both emotionally and unexpectedly: I consequently wrote a letter to her after this event to tell her how deeply sorry I was and that perhaps it would be better in that event, since I had caused her this much distress, if I did not pursue our relationship any further at that time: Subsequent to that moment I have not heard another word from her or from anybody else, from that day to this.

I do accept that my behaviour was unacceptable and that contacting my sister at the time, might have helped to alleviate some of her disappointment, but I did also nurse a degree of misgiving when I was told by my sister, that an introduction to the rest of the family might proceed only after they had gained sufficient time for them all to 'get used to me': It had never been my intention, in this relationship that we were so wonderfully engaged in, at this time, to include the prerequisite of a potential rapprochement; the possibility of a future integration scenario, that might be necessary so that they might then be afforded sufficient time to become more accustomed to me first: The requirement for my family, of becoming used to me at all, had never even entered into any comprehension of what a cordial, mutually satisfactory relationship, might actually have involved.

So do I proceed in this life and so do I still have regular pauses to deal with: Solutions never come easily and neither do memories; happy ones anyway: Share that thought with me and rest quietly with all of your own new comprehensions but please do not be angry if you know what it is that awaits you as you seek for your own dreams and your own attainments: They might finally provide you with some solace in the pursuit of your own retributions: Draw some comfort if you will, from this story and thank you sincerely for all of your time and all of your attention.

Finally and most importantly, please don't ever look on this story as a poor-me kind of tale: It was never ever intended to be told to you as that: One lesson that I will always be grateful for, in all of my dealings with the Poor sisters of Nazareth, is an ability to cope with a life that became necessarily reliant on the unusual requirements of compassion and comfort, in a way that meant that personal issues could actually be dealt with, with a perfunctorily dismissive grin: This is the manner in which I have always been comfortable, in approaching this little effort and at the end of the day, isn't that also an essential ingredient in coping with the harsher lessons that life still continues to throw at us.

THE END.

Printed in Poland
by Amazon Fulfillment
Poland Sp. z o.o., Wrocław
14 March 2023

7946c926-37b1-4538-8ec5-76b40b749cc5R01